Hermann's Cohen's
Kantian Philosophy of Religion

European University Studies
Europäische Hochschulschriften
Publications Universitaires Européennes

Series XX
Philosophy

Reihe XX   Série XX
Philosophie
Philosophie

Vol./Band 679

PETER LANG
Bern · Berlin · Bruxelles · Frankfurt am Main · New York · Oxford · Wien

Ketil Bonaunet

Hermann Cohen's Kantian Philosophy of Religion

PETER LANG
Bern · Berlin · Bruxelles · Frankfurt am Main · New York · Oxford · Wien

Bibliographic information published by Die Deutsche Bibliothek
Die Deutsche Bibliothek lists this publication in the Deutsche
Nationalbibliografie; detailed bibliographic data is available on the Internet at
‹http://dnb.ddb.de›.

British Library and Library of Congress Cataloguing-in-Publication Data:
A catalogue record for this book is available from *The British Library*, Great Britain,
and from *The Library of Congress*, USA

ISSN 0721-3417
ISBN 3-03910-421-7
US-ISBN 0-8204-7033-3

© Peter Lang AG, Europäischer Verlag der Wissenschaften, Bern 2004
Hochfeldstrasse 32, Postfach 746, CH-3000 Bern 9
info@peterlang.com, www.peterlang.com, www.peterlang.net

All rights reserved.
All parts of this publication are protected by copyright.
Any utilisation outside the strict limits of the copyright law, without
the permission of the publisher, is forbidden and liable to prosecution.
This applies in particular to reproductions, translations, microfilming,
and storage and processing in electronic retrieval systems.

Printed in Germany

Acknowledgments

I wish to thank Professor Karl Ameriks and Professor P. Quinn (University of Notre Dame) for their comments on the different drafts of this essay, and for several conversations on topics relevant to the manuscript during my stay as a Visiting Scholar at Notre Dame, 2002–2003. I am also grateful to Professor Kenneth Seeskin (Northwestern University) for his written criticisms of an earlier version of this work, and to Professor Reiner Wimmer (University of Tübingen) for his comments and for his corrections of the German quotations in my manuscript. While this final version of the work does not do justice to all the points raised by these colleagues, their comments and critiques kept me from overlooking important problems in Cohen's conceptions and my interpretations of them. Finally, my deepest gratitude to Mrs. Valerie Friedline, Mishawaka, Indiana, for editing this English manuscript.

Tromsø, May 24. 2004   Ketil Bonaunet

Contents

I. Introduction: Some general remarks
   on Kantian philosophy of religion
   and a first approach to Cohen 9

   1. On "Kantian philosophy of religion" 10

   2. The three phases of Cohen's authorship;
      an overview 22

   3. General or Jewish philosophy of religion? 26

II. Cohen's Kantian philosophy of religion 29

   1. Religion, logic and aesthetics 29

   2. Messianism and the "God of ethics" 32

   3. Compassion (Mitleid) and the complementation
      of ethics by a religious consciousness 37

      The "ethical" concept of the human being 38

      The discovery of the "thou" and the necessity
      of transcending ethics 46

      The fact of suffering within human existence 49

      The Jewish prophets and "the discovery
      of the fellow human being" 52

Compassion and recognition
of the "concrete Other" 57

A preliminary assessment 47

Compassion and the problem
of transcending ethics 64

4. Moral guilt as problem in a Kantian philosophy
of religion 73

On guilt as a problem of ethics 73

N. Hartmann on consciousness of guilt 79

The problem of the possibility
of moral regeneration – Kant and Cohen 82

Knowledge of guilt, liberation from guilt
and the "problem of the individual" 90

The phenomenology of the knowledge of- and
redemption from from guilt (Cohen and Scheler) ... 104

Confession of guilt as a "speech act" 109

Cohen on penance and suffering.
(A (failed) theodicé) 110

The problem of guilt, the irreducibility
of the individual and the legitimacy of religion 114

5. Cohen and the autonomy of religion 131

Literature 147

Index 163

I. Introduction: Some general remarks on Kantian philosophy of religion and a first approach to Cohen

Within the plurality of investigations in the philosophy of religion one can distinguish between two main approaches. One is theoretical-philosophical. This approach is first of all characteristic for traditional "natural theology", in which one in different ways seeks arguments for (or later in the history of philosophy also against) God's existence, and seeks to clarify God's nature and essential attributes.

Another main approach in the philosophy of religion is of a practical-philosophical kind. A practical-philosophical approach is characteristic for what we could designate as, in a broad sense, Kantian philosophy of religion. I will on the following pages first try to explicate generally the conception of a Kantian philosophy of religion. Later in this essay I will give a more extensive exposition and carry out a more thorough investigation and evaluation of some central aspects of Hermann Cohen's version of a Kantian philosophy of religion, primarily as it is formulated in Cohen's two last works: Begriff der Religion im System der Philosophie (1915) (BR) and Religion der Vernunft aus den Quellen des Judentums (posthumous 1919) (RV). Even though my exploration will concentrate on Cohen's philosophy of religion, some of Kant's perspectives will also be treated, where this is relevant, for the discussion of Cohen's thought.

1. On "Kantian" philosophy of religion

Kantian philosophy of religion rejects the possibility of theoretical proofs for or against the existence of the transcendent being (or in K. Rahner's words: "the abyss of mystery") we call God. A critical philosophy, recognizing its own limits, realizes that we have no reason to assert that the limits of being must be identical with the limits of our empirical or rational knowledge (cf. Lutz-Bachmann 1996 p. 77, Köhler 1996 p. 134). The idea that there is a reality beyond these limits "hat nichts Abwegiges an sich" (Kutschera 1991 p. 254). And a presumptive metaphysical or even "scientific" atheism, rejecting the being of God or declaring it to be impossible, is in contradiction to fundamental principles of a critical philosophy and transcends its limits. But at the same time, neither can God's existence be object for any objective-theoretical knowledge. This approach opens, as Kant says, space for a genuine faith. As Kant says:

> Ich kann [...] Gott, Freiheit und Unsterblichkeit zum Behuf des notwendigen praktischen Gebrauchs meiner Vernunft nicht einmal *annehmen*, wenn ich nicht der spekulativen Vernunft zugleich ihre Anmassung überschwenglicher Einsichten *benehme* [...]. Ich musste also das *Wissen* aufheben, um zum *Glauben* Platz zu bekommen (KRV B xxx).

However, the *quid-iuris*-question is essential in Kantian philosophy, and correspondingly, also in Kantian philosophy of religion[1]: The legitimacy of our claims of knowledge and of ethics must be subjected to transcendental investigation, and – possibly – be justified in a "transcendental deduction". And correspondingly: Any religion

---

1   According to Cohen's interpretation of Kant, the *quid-iuris*-question is the basic question for Kant's philosophical enterprise in its entirety (cf. Ollig 1979 p. 31).

claiming validity must be subjected to investigation by critical reason, and defend its legitimacy. Religion must, as Cohen says, show its "legitimacy and value" by being able to present itself as a "religion of reason" (RV 5 and 39). In this respect religious faith is, according to a Kantian philosophy of religion, not a phenomenon beyond any rational-philosophical approach.

As the different main kinds of the sciences (Wissenschaften) are "given" as objects for a "transcendental deduction" (in Cohen's comprehensive system of philosophy: the natural sciences within "pure logics", and jurisprudence and the *Geisteswissenschaften* in connection with the transcendental legitimation of ethics), so art and religion are also "given" as phenomena of culture that philosophy must investigate concerning their legitimacy: "Es darf nicht hier anders vonstatten gehen, als es mit allen Grundmächten der Kultur ergangen ist. Von ihrer Faktizität gehen wir aus und fragen daruthin nach ihrem Rechte" (BR 8). The question of the justificatory ground (Rechtsgrund) for the existence and preservation of religion must then be explored in a transcendental investigation.

The task of critical philosophy is not to construct a new rational religion: Religion is a fact; it is already there. And a critical philosophy of religion is, in the same way as the other philosophical disciplines, transcendentally-methodically committed to a *factum* (cf. Holzhey 2000 p. 46). Already Kant himself emphasizes how his concern is not about any philosophical construction of a rational religion. Religion is "given", as is also the "fact of experience". And the task is, insofar as religion already is present (i.e. for Kant primarily Christianity), to investigate whether its contents can be rationally defended and upheld or conserved "within the limits of reason" (Kant: SF, VII, 6 n and Rel. B xxi; cf. Kvist 1890 p. 245 f.). Correspondingly, Cohen poses the question of how far religion, as it is existing, can be said to have a "share in reason" (Cohen: RV 8). In agreement with this conception, an interpretation of the "sources of Judaism" is a central concern for Cohen.

Kant's idea of a conservation of religious contents within the "limits of reason" or Cohen's idea of showing religion's "share in reason" and its character of a "religion of reason" needs, however, to be clarified.

(1) First, there is a question about the character of the relevant "religious contents". According to some of Kant's ways of expression, his aim seems to be a rational justification of theoretical-metaphysical judgments of the existence of God, even if they don't imply claims of knowledge and only are supported by practical-philosophical arguments.[2] In this respect, Kant's philosophy of religion could be understood as a continuation of traditional "natural theology", insofar as Kant seeks to establish proofs of God's existence, even if they are based on moral arguments only. And Kant's doctrine of the postulate of God's existence could be read as exemplifying yet another way – a "sixth way" – i. e. in addition to Thomas Aquinas' *quinque viae*, (cf. Aquinas: ST I, q.1, a.3), and as a "moral proof of the existence of God".

A rational justification of religious faith has to include, in some way, support for some propositions of the existence and nature of God, or something correponding to this, insofar as religious faith implies claiming that some such propositions are true, or, in other words, insofar as some "doxastic" components are essential for religious faith (cf. Kutschera 1991 p. 245). In connection with faith, Kant also talks about *"Fürwahrhalten"* (cf. e. g. KRV B 850 f. and KPV A 255). The objects of religious faith are according to Kant, as we already suggested, not accessible through theoretical knowledge, but there is nonetheless a question about our *"Fürwahrhalten"* of

---

2   Cf. Kant's definition of the concept of a "postulate", as "einen *theoretischen*, als solchen aber nicht erweislichen Satz […], so fern er einem apriori unbedingt geltenden *praktischen* Gesetze unzertrennlich anhängt" (KPV A 220).

some relevant propositions (cf. KdU, V, 471 f.). This does not, however, imply that the philosophy of religion could be adequately reduced to an "epistemology of religious belief", and that the *quid iuris*-question concerning religion should turn out to be identical with the question of the legitimacy of asserting propositions of God's existence and nature. As Kant himself emphasizes, "Glauben [...] bloss in der Bedeutung eines theoretischen Fürwahrhaltens [...] ist [...] kein Stück der Religion" (Kant: SF, VII, 42). The "doxastic" components primarily ought to serve our ethical practice. Characteristic to Kant's philosophical approach to religious faith is further that the critical question is posed in terms of an attitude of hope, and that hope constitutes the fundamental category of religion and philosophy of religion.[3] And hope in this context, is to be understood more as a disposition or an attitude towards some essential elements of our ethical practice, than as something that concerns a set of theoretical judgments.

According to Cohen the problem for a critical philosophy of religion is, as we have suggested above, the legitimacy of religion as a "fact of culture". And this fact of culture consists not primarily of a complex of theoretical judgments or beliefs, but includes a comprehensive set of attitudes, ethical and ritual practices and institutions.[4] So, the task for Cohen's Kantian philosophy of religion is to provide a rational justification for our participation in such a complex of beliefs, attitudes and practices.

---

[3] Cf. (e. g.) KRV B 833 where Kant poses the three fundamental questions of a critical philosophy: the theoretical "Was kann ich wissen?", the ethical "Was soll ich tun?", and the religious "Was darf ich hoffen?". – These are according to Kant, however, constituent parts of the most fundamental problem of philosophy: "Was ist der Mensch?" (cf. Logik, IX, 25).

[4] For a brief survey of the different elements of religion, see e. g. Ringgren/Ström 1972 p. 12 f.

Cohen's point of departure for an understanding of religion, i.e. of religion as a "fact of culture", clearly implies transcending a conception of philosophy of religion as primarily occupied with the "epistemology of religion". Religion concerns, as Cohen says, "ein Gesamtbilde des menschlichen Lebens". "Diese einheitliche Ganzheit wird bezeichnet durch den Weg" (RV 240). And as G. Haeffner – in line with this – points out: "Was immer Religion sonst sein mag, so ist sie doch sicher [...] eine Praxis, ein Weg [...]. Statt von einem "Weg" kann man auch von einer zielorientierten "Lebensform" sprechen" (Haeffner 1997 p. 175). The "doxastic" elements in religion then serve primarily this "way", as a practice or a religious "form of life" (cf. ibid. p. 177). It would, therefore, I think, in no way be inadequate if one, parallel to talking of a "fact of culture" as according to Cohen's way of expression, makes use of the (neo-)Wittgensteinian concept of a "form of life" (cf. Kutschera 1991 p. 212 and Clack 1999 p. 87 ff.) also to express Cohen's concerns. As I understand it, it is also reasonable to assert that this orientation, i.e. towards religion as a "form of life", is strengthened in Cohen's philosophy of religion, in relation to Kant, because of his point of departure in religion as a "fact of culture", and that Cohen's philosophy of religion, correspondingly, more pronouncedly stands out as what Haeffner designates as "eine Religionsphilosophie, die sich nicht primär auf eine [...] Theologie, sondern auf die Religion als Lebensform bezieht" (Haeffner, 1997 p. 196). Further, in this respect, I think Cohen's philosophy of religion represents a more promising basis for exploring some fundamental problems, within a, still Kantian-critical, viable approach to the philosophy of religion. A religious "form of life", however, ought to be conceived of in such a way that it is not thought of as a "form of life" in which a person participates *besides* or along with other "forms of life". This constitutes, as is well known, a common criticism of some traits of the "neo-Wittgensteinian" philosophy of religion, which attempt to explore religion just in terms of the concept of a "form of life".[5] Rather, the religious "form of life" ought to be seen as a kind of "over-arching" practice, which partly includes and partly "colors" the other "forms of life" in which one participates, and through and in which one realizes one's human existence.

One characteristic trait of Cohen's philosophy of religion is his insistence that religion has a "peculiarity" (Eigenart) in relation to the other areas of human culture, such as science, morality and art, but no "selfsubsistence" (Selbständigkeit). These three "areas of culture" correspond respectively to the disciplines of logic, ethics and aesthetics in Cohen's system of philosophy, disciplines in which he carries out transcendental-philosophical investigations of the conditions of validity for each of these "facts of culture" (cf. Holzhey 2000 p. 44). These tri-part "areas of culture" and disciplines of philosophy are further connected with three "fundamental orientations" or "directions" (Richtungen) in the human consciousness: thought, will, and feeling. These three "fundamental directions" of consciousness come to expression in religion. And a philosophical legitimation of religion must according to Cohen correspondingly be connected with each of the three main parts of the systematical totality structure of philosophy, i.e. both logic, ethics and aesthetics. The contents of

---

5   The critics commonly assert that this is a philosophy of religion that "seeks to divide religion from other life-forms as independent and self-sufficient, immune from criticism and incapable of being evangelized [...]" (H. Palmer, here after Schaeffler 1999 p. 82). – For an overview of persons and positions within neo-wittgensteinian philosophy of religion, see Clack 1999, Chapter 4. – This criticism, however, does not apply to Wittgenstein's own ideas of the philosophy of religion. As R. Wimmer has shown in several works in which he elaborates the potential of Wittgenstein's thought with regard to some fundamental problems of the philosophy of religion, the religious understanding of our existence according to Wittgenstein aims at encompassing the whole of our existence and life, – "das Ganze des Daseins, das Leben in seiner Totalität" (Wimmer 1992 p. 95), and within the context of an experience of the world in its totality (cf. ibid. p. 108).

religion must be explained in continuity, or as Cohen says, in *homogenity*, with these, and as a dimension that represents a complementation (Ergänzung) of each of them. Of course, we cannot already so early in our investigation draw any final conclusion concerning the viability of Cohen's idea that religion has a "peculiarity", but no "selfsubsistence", in relation to the other "areas of culture" and their corresponding philosophical system parts. But Cohen's conception, even if it first appears to represent a weakness in his understanding of religion, on further reflection, it appears to be of importance, insofar as religion is thereby understood as a "form of life" that hangs together with the other dimensions of the human existence. On the contrary, insisting on the "selfsubsistence" of religion, could imply that religion is separated from the other forms of life, as self-sufficient and independent of them (cf. note 5 above).[6] – Besides that, Cohen's idea of the connection of religion with the different other parts of his system of philosophy, demonstrates that he does not consider religion a "transitory element of human culture" (cf. Dreyer 1985 p. 217) or something a better understanding and a more "advanced" age could do without. For him, a religious "form of life" does not represent a stage that ought to be transcended.

(2) In addition there is a question of how the idea of the "share of reason" of the contents of religion should be understood. In this respect, it is an essential concern for Cohen in his later works that the philosophical justification of religion ought not to imply a "suspension" or *Aufhebung* of the notions of religion into an immanent philosophical conception or discourse. Cohen himself raises some doubt about whether Kant's project of philosophy of religion avoids

---

6   H. Holzey points out how Cohen's standpoint in this respect, i. e. the rejection of the "self-subsistence" of religion also implies that fundamentalism is bereft of its ground (cf. Holzhey 2001 p. 9, n. 19). This is a point of considerable importance for a philosophy of religion for our time

endangering the peculiarity (Eigenart) of religion: "[...] der Wert von Kants Charakteristik der Religion besteht in der Ethiko-Theologie, mit der jedoch die Gefahr verbunden ist, dass die Religion in Ethik aufgeht und ihre Eigenart verliert" (BR 94).

H. Scholz, who worked on problems of the philosophy of religion partly at the same time as Cohen, and who, at least occasionally, formulated his questions and positions in Cohen's language, credits Kant with an adequate understanding of a peculiarity (Eigenart) on behalf of religion, for religion is according to Kant "durchaus von der Moralität verschieden" (Scholz 1922 p. 82). But he blames Kant for depriving religion of its "selfsubsistence": "Die Autonomie der Religion geht [...] verloren. Die Religion erwächst nicht auf eigenem Grunde, sondern [...] auf dem Boden der Moralität. Sie ist eine Konsequenz der Moral und nur dieses" (Scholz 1922 p. 83). It can hardly be denied that there are some strong reductionistic tendencies in Kant's philosophy of religion, and perhaps especially in his Streit der Fakultäten, where Kant unambiguously claims that all "faith of church" (Kirchenglaube) must be transformed into a "pure faith of reason" (Vernunftglaube) (SF, VII, 42) (see concerning this Ricken 1992 p. 185 and 189).[7] But Kant concedes that a religion within the limits of reason also must include an open attitude towards some "parerga" (cf. Rel. B 63 f.), i.e. conceptions that transcend reason, without, however, contradicting reason, and which are at the boundary of reason. Kant remarks in this respect that we, on philosophical foundations, can admit "workings of grace", but, however, as something that is in itself incomprehensible and resistant to rational explication (cf. Byrne 1998 p. 58). And Kant – and a Kantian philosophy of religion – must be said to be justified in

---

7 Cf. also R. Wimmer's remark that: "Der autonome und der übervernünftige Charakter der lebendigen Religiösität kann in Kant's Konzeption nicht begriffen werden. Darauf beruht ihre Fragwürdigkeit und Begrenztheit" (Wimmer 1990 p. 13).

this notion, i.e. that this is a point at which philosophy reaches its limit. At the same time, it must be admitted that there exists a certain tension in Kant's conception concerning the problem of an acknowledgement of autonomous religious contents (cf. Habichler 1991 p. 44 ff.).

I will however defend the view that Kantian philosophy, at least in Cohen's version, clearly is open for an idea that J. Habermas considers to be characteristic for the relation to religion according to a "post-metaphysical" philosophy, namely that philosophy in itself is not able "sich das, wovon im religiösen Diskurs die Rede ist, [...] *als* religiöse Erfahrungen zu eigen (zu) machen" (Habermas 1991 a p. 136) or to completely translate the original ("originäre") contents of religious experience "ins Medium der begründeten Rede", and that philosophy neither could replace nor displace, but has to respect and co-exist (anerkennend koexistieren) with religion (cf. Lutz-Bachmann 1996 p. 77). The phenomena of living religiosity cannot *qua* such be appropriated by a philosophical argumentative reason. And the task for a critical-Kantian philosophy of religion must, in other words, be formulated such that its concern is

> die Andersartigkeit des spezifischen Glaubensinhalts im Medium der begründenden Rede und diskursiv verfahrender Rationalität einzuholen, ohne diesen dabei jedoch zu beschädigen oder in seinem mit Vernunft nicht identischen Potential aufzuheben (Lutz-Bachmann 1996 a p. 186 f.),

in so far as one acknowledges that there is no relation of identity between, on the one hand, what is rationally justifiable and in this respect has a "share in reason" and, on the other, what *is* rational (cf. Schnädelbach 1985 p. 85).[8]

Cohen rejects explicitly in his later works the notion he formerly held of a reduction of religion to ethics or a "dissolution"

---

8   H. M. Baumgartner distinguishes in this respect (correspondingly) between "Rationabilität" and "Rationalität" (cf. Baumgartner 1992 p. 167).

(Auflösung) of religion into ethics (cf. BR 42),[9] and defends what he designates as the "peculiarity" of religion. Whether this implies a sufficient preservation of a transrational dimension in religion, in continuity with the rational, and of the autonomy of the contents of religion with respect to an adequate philosophy of religion, *versus* a reductionistic philosophy of religion, must be one of the decisive questions in our investigation of Cohen's ideas (see below p. 131 ff.).

The investigation of the legitimacy of religion must, insofar as theoretical reason is insufficient for this task, be based on a practical rationality. The decisive contribution of a Kantian approach within the philosophy of religion is concrete elaborations of attempts of a practical-philosophical legitimation or justification of religious faith and practice (cf. Kutschera 1991 p. viii). At a first glance the rejection of a theoretical-demonstrative approach to the problem of the rational legitimacy of religion seems to imply a considerable weakening, as compared to the alleged contributions of traditional natural theology. However, by reflection we will soon realize how the, in a certain sense, *weaker* claims of a Kantian approach in certain respects implies a strength, namely insofar as the attempts to grasp or seize the existence of God by rational *proofs*, from the standpoint of religious faith, could be said to represent a promethean *hybris* on behalf of finite human beings: God as the "completely Other" (das ganz Andere), and furthermore God's existence, cannot be an object for any objective-theoretical human knowledge and certainty. We should note how, as R. Wimmer states, a successful proof of God's existence would imply a transformation of faith to knowledge, or "die Aufhebung des Glaubens in Wissen". Wimmer further remarks that: "[…] eine solche Verblendung (erscheint mir) die Folge menschlicher Eigenmächtigkeit zu sein, die den Glauben an Gott

---

9 Cohen states explicitly and unambiguously that religion ought to be "suspended" or "changed" into ethics, both in ERW (58) and in RuS (151 and 158).

[...] unter die eigene Verfügung zu bringen trachtet" (Wimmer 1992 p. 96 f.).[10]

Further, the practical-philosophical approach characteristic to a Kantian philosophy of religion could be said to possess the merit that

10   In a certain sense we can also see the point of R. Löw's assertion, within the context of his rejection of "Die neuen Gottesbeweise", that a logically successful and compelling proof of God's existence, would imply a blasphemy: For no finite existing being can transparently see through (ergründen) God, and compel him to a revelation of His existence (cf. Löw 1994 p. 196). – There is however a question whether the traditional so-called proofs of God's existence really have been meant to have the status of *proofs*. Concerning Anselm's ontological proof of God's existence, R. Wimmer has proposed a reading that emphasizes its character as an act of profession of faith (see Wimmer 1991). And concerning Aquinas' five ways a number of commentators have asserted that it is against his own intention to present them as proofs, and that "St. Thomas with his [...] five ways only wanted to explain that belief in God has a rational foundation and is [...] intelligible to human beings. [...] however this is not proof of the existence of God" (Schillebeeckx 1994 p. 56). So there is attached an act of faith to each of the five ways (cf. the conclusion of the respective paragraphs in the Summa Theologiae (ST I, q. 2, a. 3): "[...] and this we call God" (in different formulations). To support a reading like this one could refer to ST II–II, 2, 10, ad 2, where Aquinas explicitly states that the reasons that are adduced for "the authority of faith" are not *demonstrationes*, but that they remove obstacles for faith (*impedimenta fidei*) by showing that there is nothing impossible in what belongs to faith (cf. Ricken 1995 p. 290 f.). Anyway, this interpretation is disputed, and, among others, B. Davies rejects such a reading of Aquinas, referring to textual evidence according to which Aquinas in this respect talks about "demonstrative arguments" (cf. Davies 1993 p. 22). – Further, it is, however, interesting and, I think, important to note how also Aquinas emphasizes a practical-philosophical approach to religious faith, insofar as he connects the transition to a religious attitude to the human life to transcending the imperfect happiness accessible to a merely philosophical understanding (see ST I–II, q. 1–5); (see concerning this also Bonaunet 2002 p. 117 ff.). To be sure, the point of connection here is not morality in the more restricted Kantian sense, but the – in a wider sense – ethical question of what a human life ought to consist in (cf. Donagan 1999 p. 194).

the question of the legitimacy of religion is the object of reflection within a context where this question is existentially relevant for a human being, i.e. the context of his/her moral existence and the problem of the meaning of morality, and in certain respects where philosophy in itself cannot give any "consolation", as Habermas remarks, and which concern negative anthropological ground phenomena, as guilt, "das unvermeidliche Leid und das nicht-gesühnte Unrecht, die Kontingenzen von Not, Einsamkeit, Krankheit und Tod", on which religion sheds a new light "und ertragen lehrt" (Habermas 1991 b p. 125; cf. also Ricken 1992 p. 193). In accordance with this kind of context as *locus* for the reflection of philosophy of religion, Kant understands God's essential being, – insofar as an understanding here is possible at all,[11] in personalistic terms, and this means in terms that are relevant for our practical concerns as human beings (cf. Fischer 1995 p. 352 f.; see e.g. KPV A 224 ff., 236 n and 252). In this respect N. Fischer points out how Kant leaves behind physical and physicalistic explanations as a basis for the approach to the problem of the existence of God, and instead searches for an approach where our moral existence as human beings constitutes the point of departure, and how

> ihm deshalb moralistische Engführungen vorzuwerfen, ist anachronistisch. Passender ist der Versuch, den *Wandel von physikalisch zu personal fundierten Kategorien im philosophischen Gottdenken* wahrzunehmen, der bei Kant unabgeschlossen sein mag, zu dem er aber doch seinen Beitrag geleistet hat (Fischer 1995 p. 353).[12]

11 Cf. Kant's assertion "dass uns das höchste Wesen nach demjenigen, was es an sich selbst sei, gänzlich unerforschlich und auf bestimmte Weise so gar undenkbar sei" (Prol. A 178 f.).
12 Concerning Kant's reorientation with regard to the concept of God, away from an abstract-theoretical knowledge, cf. also Wood 1992 p. 403: "His plain intent is that the moral arguments should serve as a kind of substitute for the theoretical proofs rejected by his theoretical critique; only what they are supposed to justify is a warm and living religious faith, as distinct from dead, abstract theoretical knowledge".

And Cohen emphasizes that:

> Nur in Korrelation zum Menschen soll das Wesen Gottes bestimmbar werden. Nur diejenigen Attribute sollen ihm zuerteilt werden dürfen, welche die Sittlichkeit des Menschen begründen, seine Annäherung an Gott begünstigen (BR 106; see also RV 187 f.).

Corresponding to this, according to Cohen's fundamental conception the correlation God–man is the constitutive moment of religion (as we will explore in more detail later in this essay). This approach to the philosophy of religion is characteristic for Cohen as a Kantian philosopher of religion. On the contrary, Thomas Aquinas' "five ways" unambiguously take mediaeval physics as their point of departure (cf. O'Meara 1997 p. 91). As is well known, it has not been easy to establish the existence of the "God of the philosophers". But even if one could succeed in this, there remain considerable difficulties with carrying out the next, decisive step, from the concept of the "God of the philosophers" to faith in a God, having meaning and importance for a human existence on earth (cf. Löw 1994 p. 195). A Kantian approach to the question of the rationality and legitimacy might then, as I will propose, be said to be closer to an explication of the religious believers' own reasons for their faith, or the "ordinary believer's actual, operative, reasons for belief" (Gutting 1982 p. 6).

2. The three phases of Cohen's authorship; an overview

(Also) with regard to Cohen there has been an extensive discussion concerning the relations between his later and his earlier philosophy – a discussion that is still ongoing and unsettled – and about whether an "existential-ontological" or a "methodological-idealistic" interpretation of his late philosophy of religion is the most adequate (cf. Ollig 1979 a p. 230). – There are three main periods of Cohen's authorship. To the first period belong his commentaries on Kant's philosophy (extensive commentaries on Kant's theory of knowledge, ethics and aesthetics).[13] "Das Prinzip der Infinitesimalmethode" (1883) prepares the elaboration of his own comprehensive "system of philosophy", in its three parts or *Glieder*: Logik der reinen Erkenntnis (1902), Ethik des reinen Willens (1904) (ERW) and Ästhetik des reinen Gefühls (1912). These cover what Cohen refers to as the three "areas" within human "culture", and correspond to the three basic "directions of consciousness": thinking, will and feeling, as, according to Cohen, all parts of the system are supported of corresponding "kinds of consciousness" ("Alle Systemglieder werden durch entsprechende Arten des Bewusstseins getragen") (BR 44). – Besides there is, beginning with "Ein Bekenntnis in der Judenfrage" in 1880, always in Cohen's authorship a kind of "under-current", a number of smaller writings on Jewish themes.[14]

The first two periods of Cohen's authorship fall within his nearly forty years of work in Marburg (from 1873 to 1912), where P. Natorp also worked from 1880 until his death in 1924. With his emeritation in July 1912, Cohen moved to Berlin where, until his

---

13 Kants Theorie der Erfahrung (1871), Kants Begründung der Ethik (1877) and Kants Begründung der Ästhetik (1889).
14 Edited in Jüdische Schriften (3 volumes, 1924). Among Cohen's fundamental concerns belongs also the idea of a synthesis of "Judentum" and "Deutschtum", in terms of the German "Humanitätstradition" (from Kant, Lessing, Schiller and others) (see e. g. Cohen's "Über das Eigentümliche des deutschen Geistes" (1914)). His optimism and hopes in this regard stand in sharp opposition already to the anti-semitic attitudes he himself encountered in different situations, but especially to the fact that his (at that time) 82-years old widow Martha Cohen was killed in the concentration camp of Theresienstadt in 1942.

death in 1918, he worked at a Jewish institution of education (which became the "Akademie für die Wissenschaft des Judentums" in 1919). During these years, Cohen published BR (1915), while RV was edited posthumously in 1919.

The question whether there is a break or continuity between Cohen's later philosophy of religion and his earlier system of philosophy is identical with the question of whether his philosophy of religion in BR and RV represents a departure from Marburg neo-Kantianism. In any case, as its title already reveals, BR can reasonably be said to be a work of transition (cf. Poma 1996 p. 9 and 29), and the question of a possible break with the Marburg-school and "system philosophy" concerns in the first instance RV. The extreme positions in this discussion are represented by F. Rosenzweig and A. Altmann respectively. According to Rosenzweig, Cohen's late philosophy, and especially RV, constitutes a "new thinking" ("ein neues Denken") and manifests a "turning towards the concrete human being" or, as U. Hommes characterizes this position: "ein Rückgang auf die konkrete Faktizität des menschlichen Daseins" (U. Hommes, here after Holzhey 1994 p. 18), which absolutely transcends Cohen's neo-Kantian – idealistic framework (cf. Rosenzweig 1994 (1924), especially p. 143f.). K. Löwith gives expression to a similar standpoint, asserting that:

> Cohen hat sich von den Grundbegriffen seines Systems […] zunächst im Begriff der Religion behutsam und dann, in der Religion der Vernunft, entschieden gelöst. […] Das grosse Alterswerk […] beginnt, womit die Ethik abschloss: mit Gott, mit der Einzigkeit Gottes, und handelt sodann von Schöpfung und Offenbarung, von der Entdeckung des Andern und Fremden als Mitmenschen, von Versöhnung und messianischer Zukunftserwartung […], vom Gebet, um mit dem Frieden als Endziel der leidvollen Menschengeschichte zu schliessen (Löwith 1968 p. 371).

On the other hand, Altmann tries to show how the basic ideas in RV, and especially the conception of a "correlation between God and the human being" and a corresponding "correlation human being – human being", in connection with which Cohen's thoughts on the "facticity" of the "concrete" human being are formulated (see below), must be seen in continuity with his ("old") "system thinking" (cf. Altmann 1994 (1962)). In these controversies D. Adelmann represents a mediating position (see Adelmann 1994 (1968)).

Recently K. Wuchterl has expressed an opinion which seems to come very close to Rosenzweig's:

> Das Spätwerk Cohens fällt ganz offensichtlich aus dem Rahmen des neukantianischen Denkens […]. Zugleich nimmt er […] im Rückgang auf die nackte Existenz der endlichen Kreatur Gedanken Heideggers vorweg (Wuchterl 1995 p. 116 (referring to BR)).

On the contrary A. Poma (1997 p. 157 ff.) and D. Novak (2000 p. 226 and 229 f.) both argue against Rosenzweig's position.

I will not, however, occupy myself with this discussion beyond the preceding summary of the different opinions. My aim is to try to extract insights from Cohen's late philosophy which, I believe, may be important contributions to understanding certain fundamental problems of ethics and the philosophy of religion, and their interrelations. And, insofar as ethics according to Cohen's conception is to be understood as "a doctrine of the human being", "eine Lehre vom Menschen" (cf. e.g. RV 13 ff.; see also ERW, Einleitung), and religion shall be a continuation and completion of ethics, my concern will be a reading of Cohen's texts with the aim of finding contributions to a more adequate articulation of our self-understanding as human beings. My reading, however, is built on the presupposition that Cohen's late philosophy takes care of what H. Holzhey talks about as the commitment of philosophy to the reality of life (Lebenswirklichkeit) of the concrete human being (cf. Holzhey 1994 p. 16). Whether Cohen's philosophy here breaks away from, or is in continuity with his system of philosophy is a matter of less importance for our purposes. Perhaps R. Wiehl's conclusion is the most adequate with regard to this problem: "(es) bleibt bei genauerer Betrachtung schliesslich offen, ob überhaupt eine Veränderung der ursprünglichen Systematik vorliegt oder ob nur eine Klärung, die Korrektur einer bisherigen Unbestimmtheit vollzogen wird" (Wiehl 2000 p. 403).

3. General or Jewish philosophy of religion?

Already here in the introduction we must, however, focus on a distinctive feature of the method in Cohen's late philosophy, which is especially conspicuous in RV: Cohen's contributions to an understanding of our *conditio humana* appear through a reconstruction of what he designates as religion's "share in reason", and by extensive interpretations of "the sources of Judaism" (the Pentateuch, the Prophets and the Psalms, in addition to Mischna/Talmud). This does not imply, however, that it is necessary to read Cohen's late philosophy as exclusively or primarily a Jewish philosophy, i.e. in the sense of "a philosophy *of* Judaism" (cf. Seeskin 1990 p. 3), nor will I do so. For as K. Seeskin remarks: "A person may follow Herman Cohen in using Jewish sources, but this does not mean, nor did Cohen intend it to mean, that the conclusions are parochial in nature" (ibid.). Cohen's concern is, as I have already suggested, to reconstruct material from Judaism as *rational-philosophical* insights, as contributions to an understanding of or a "doctrine of the human being" (cf. RV 13 ff.) and to an explication of the concept of a "religion of reason", i.e. as a religious form of life that can be shown to be rationally legitimate. Thus one can see the real importance of Cohen's late philosophy in his thematization of some of the basic problems in modern philosophy of religion in general (cf. Ollig 1979 a p. 329).

There exist readings of Cohen's late philosophy which primarily or exclusively understand it as a Jewish philosophy of religion, or also "more" or "essentially" as a Jewish theology.[15] In line with this kind of understanding, E. Goodman-Thau refers to Cohen's *"Spätwerk"* as a Jewish philosophy of religion, "die im Grunde ein Entwurf einer religiösen Hermeneutik aus den Quellen des Judentums darstellt" (Goodman-Thau 2000 p. 167). Readings like this have, to a considerable degree, been dominating, in connection with a corresponding polarization within the *"Wirkungsgeschichte"* after Cohen, according to which philosophers generally have been occupied with investigating Cohen's interpretations of Kant and his own neo-Kantian philosophy, and for whom his works in the philosophy of religion have been of little or no importance, while his latest works, first and foremost, have been studied in Jewish religious circles (cf. Holzhey 2000, xi and p. 37 ff.).[16]

While I do not intend to underestimate the importance of Cohen's hermeneutical efforts with the "sources of Judaism", in line with K. Seeskin's and H. L. Ollig's approach to Cohen (see above), and also H. Holzhey's (cf. Holzhey 2000 p. 37 f.), my exposition and discussion will proceed in accordance with Cohen's statement that: "Wir wollen [...] das allgemein Menschliche der Religion zu erkennen suchen" (BR 118). In connection with this I will also focus attention on Cohen's explicit pronouncement that Judaism alone does not constitute "*die* Religion der Vernunft" (ital. KB), but that other (monotheistic) religions have "share in reason", – even if he claims a special "originality" ("Ursprünglichkeit") for "the sources

---

15 Cf. D. Novak's statement on Cohen: "[...] in seinem letzten Buch, wo er nicht nur als Philosoph, sondern sogar mehr als ein jüdischer Theologe schreibt" (Novak 2000 p. 226), and also on RV that: "es handelt wesentlich vom Judentum" (ibid. p. 239).
16 Of course there are exceptions in this regard, as e.g. H. O. Ollig's works (1978, 1979 and 1979 a).

of Judaism", as a "primary source" (Urquell) for other sources of a "religion of reason" (cf. RV 8 ff. and 39 f.). But his main idea implies that "[…] der Oberbegriff der Vernunft eröffnet die Aussicht, dass sich eine Mehrheit von Religionen unter ihm sammeln kann" (RV 39).[17]

---

17 – *versus* D. Novak who poses the question: "Könnte man bei Cohen an eine andere "Religion der Vernunft" als das Judentum denken?" in a way which, I think, indicates that he means that the answer must be negative (cf. Novak 2000 p. 239). Against Novak's opinion we should also note Cohen's remarks on the inescapable value of religious tolerance: "[…] ohne diesen Horizont der literarischen Humanität gibt es für den gelehrten und gebildeten Menschen keine wahrhafte Religiosität. Die Meinung von der Absolutheit der eigenen Religion ist aus dem Standpunkt der wissenschaftlichen Bildung Aberglaube" (ERW 317).

II. Cohen's Kantian philosophy of religion

1. Religion, logic and aesthetics

The connection between religion and what he designates as "logic" Cohen finds in a certain homogenity between philosophical thinking of "being", from Eleatic and Platonic roots, and the understanding of God as Being in Jewish religion: "Dem eleatischen Sein entspricht in der Religion der Begriff des einzigen Gottes, als des einzigen Seins" (BR 26). God reveals himself to the (reflective) religious mind as unique ("einzig") and incommensurable with all existing things, and as *Being* (*Sein*) in relation to all "reality" ("Wirklichkeit") and all *existence* (*Dasein*).[18] In his reading of Exodus, the second book of Moses, in chapter three, Cohen states that:

> Der Text macht es unbestreitbar, dass das Wesen des einzigen Gottes in diesem Begriff des Seins gelegt wird. Und so ist es nicht zu verwundern, dass die religiöse Spekulation über Gott und seine Einheit gebunden bleiben musste an das Problem des Seins (BR 22; cf. also RV 49 ff.).

According to Cohen, however, the fundamental idea of monotheism does not consist in maintaining that there is one God and in defending the oneness and undivided simplicity of God. The decisive moment is God's "Einzigkeit", his "uniqueness" – "schlechthin seine *Identität* mit dem Sein, so dass dieser gegenüber kein anderes

---

18 R. Wiehl points out how Cohen by this already formulates what M. Heidegger later refers to as the ontological difference between "Sein" and "Seiendes" (see Wiehl 1998 p. 156).

Sein in Geltung bleibt" (BR 26; cf. also 23 and 27, and RV 47 f.). It is in this connection between the understanding of "being" in religion and philosophy that we in Cohen's philosophy of religion have to search for what corresponds to the "doxastic" components in the proofs for God's existence in traditional natural theology, insofar as Cohen, who in ERW still talks about God's *Dasein*, (ERW 53), in his later works renounces this concept, and does not accept the adequacy of talking about God's *existence*, i.e. because God's *Sein* is the foundation of all existence (*Dasein*).[19]

The complementation or "Ergänzung" of the philosophical thinking of "being" by religion, consists, more definitely, first, in the complementation of the philosophical conception of "being" ("Sein") as "unity" ("Einheit"), by monotheism's understanding of God's being as "uniqueness" ("Einzigkeit") (cf. Wiehl 2000 p. 409 f.), and in the incommensurability between "being" in this sense and all "existence" (cf. RV 51 f.). But next: To apprehend the real meaning of monotheism we also need a transition to the categories of personality, "(eine) Verwandlung des Neutrums in die Person. [...] Gott ist nicht das Seiende und auch nicht das Eine, sondern der einzig Seiende" (RV 48 f.). This transition from an ontological "abstractum" (RV 48) to personalistic categories in terms of the philosophy of religion can be justified only by the transition from ethics to religion and the understanding of God as an ethical ideal and "archetype" or "Urbild der Sittlichkeit" (RV 187): Unless God could

---

19 Cf. P. Tillich: "If existence refers to something which can be found within the whole of reality, no divine being exists", – "existence of God [...] is in itself an impossible combination of words" (Tillich: DF p. 47). – Further, the thought of God's identity with *Sein*, in transcendence of all *Dasein*, constitutes in Cohen the fundament for a conception of religion basically in terms of negative theology, corresponding to a deep current in Jewish religious thought (from Maimonides and before, to M. Horkheimer), and also in Kant's philosophy of religion (and in Tillich).

be conceived of as person, "it would make no sense for us to strive to be like God. [...]. it is incoherent [...] that a person can strive to be like something that is impersonal, [...] that can take no action of its own" (Seeskin 2000 p. 107 f.).

Concerning religion in relation to the third main area within human culture according to Cohen's exposition, art, and the corresponding part or *"Glied"* of the system of philosophy: aesthetics, where "pure feeling" constitutes the basic category, his primary aim is to clarify what he considers to be the characteristic religious feelings or emotions, such as compassion (*Mitleid*) (see below p. 37 ff.) and longing for God (see below p. 124 f.), in contradistinction to all "feeling of art". This explication is at the same time part of his rejection of conceptions of philosophy of religion in the tradition of F. Schleiermacher, as in P. Natorp, his collegue within Marburg neo-Kantianism, where one seeks the essence of religion in an "emotion of infinity" ("Unendlichkeitsgefühl") (cf. BR 94 and 121 ff.).

It is, however, the more specific *Kantian* approach that will be the main concern of our investigation. Correspondingly, it is the connection of religion to the second part of Cohen's philosophical system, ethics, that will be the central object of our presentation and discussion of his philosophy of religion. Instead of as in traditional philosophy of religion, metaphysics, it is in Cohen's thought, as I already mentioned above, ethics, that constitutes the most important point of departure for an adequate philosophical access to the concept of religion, through a "transcendental methodics" (cf. BR 11). The ground or basis for this view lies in his conception of the philosophical-systematic centrality of ethics (cf. ERW, Einleitung).[20]

---

20 However, the Kantian elements do not, as we already have suggested, in themselves exhaust the resources of Cohen's philosophy of religion, insofar as it also includes problems which rather could be said to belong to a philosophical theology, such as the question of the "being" ("Sein") of God in contrast to the "existence" ("Dasein") of the world of creation, of God's "attributes

In accordance with his general view of the relations between the constituent parts of the system of philosophy (see above p. 15 f. and 29 ff.), neither can religion, according to Cohen, possess any "selfsubsistence" in relation to ethics. We can make a claim only of "peculiarity" ("Eigenart") on behalf of religion, insofar as it essentially concerns questions of moral relevance, which, however, in certain ways are transcending ethics. Ethics must in any case and always, in different respects as we will show below, be a foundation and precondition for religion (cf. BR 16 f.).

2. Messianism and the "God of ethics"

The doctrine of the postulates (of the existence of God and the immortality of the soul) as it is formulated in Kritik der praktischen Vernunft constitutes a central part of Kant's philosophy of religion. Cohen, however, rejects this doctrine. The rejection of eudaimonism is, according to Cohen, an essential point in Kant's ethics. But in his doctrine of the postulates, which Cohen considers one of the weakest points in Kant's philosophy, Kant, Cohen asserts, bluntly contradicts himself by letting God get the function of a "distributor" of happiness, i. e. because this doctrine is based on the concept of the "highest good" in terms of a proportionate relationship between virtue and happiness, and therefore on, according to Cohen, unjustified eudaimonistic ethical presuppositions (cf. Cohen: RH p. 79 ff.).

of action", an interpretation of the ideas of God's creation and sustaining of the world, and of the ideas of revelation, holiness and "the holy spirit". For a survey, see Poma 1997, chapter 9.

There is however in Kant's philosophy of religion another line of argumentation, leading from the concept of a "moral world" as a *regnum gratiae* in KRV (B 840), via the concept of the "kingdom of ends" in Grundlegung (Grl. 433 f.), to the concept of an "ethical commonwealth" as a "kingdom of God on earth" (cf. Rel., 3. Stück), which is not connected with any proportionalistic distribution of happiness. Kant's conception is that we have an obligation to promote this "kingdom" as a system of morally well-disposed human beings ("ein System wohlgesinnter Menschen") in relation to each other "under laws of virtue" (Rel. B 136 and 131), in which the free will (freie Willkür) of all rational beings "unter moralischen Gesetzen sowohl mit sich selbst, als mit jeder anderen Freiheit durchgängige systematische Einheit an sich hat" (KRV B 836). At the same time, however, we will see that the realization of a "kingdom" like this surpasses our capabilities as finite human beings. And this then constitutes a point of contact between philosophical ethics and the idea of a "messianic" hope for an "intervention" by a transcendent power as "a higher moral being" (Rel. B 136): "Ein moralisches Volk Gottes zu stiften, ist [...] ein Werk, dessen Ausführung nicht von Menschen, sondern nur von Gott selbst erwartet werden kann" (ibid. 141). But we can have no knowledge of what God will do to realize such a "kingdom": "(es) eröffnet sich vor (dem Menschen) der Abgrund eines Geheimnisses, von dem was Gott hiebei tue", and regarding how God will cooperate with man in this. We cannot even know whether God will do anything at all (cf. ibid. 210). But we can, and ought according to Kant, to hope for a Divine "intervention" and completion of our own strivings, while we, however, continue acting and proceeding as if all depends on ourselves and our own efforts (cf. ibid. 141).[21]

---

21 For a more extensive discussion of these matters in Kant, see Bonaunet 1993 p. 489–511, as well as 1994 a p. 10 ff.

And these are ideas Cohen elaborates further in his philosophy of religion, and which represent one of the three main routes of argumentation from ethics to the rationality of religion in his late philosophy, i.e. through which he, from the idea of how religion in certain respects can respond to some shortcomings and limitations implied by a merely immanent ethical reason, deals with the problem of the rationality and legitimacy of religion. For certain reasons I will here only briefly present this first route, before I explore the two others in more depth.

Now, this first line of argumentation in Cohen's Kantian philosophy of religion concerns hope and confidence in certain presuppositions for the realization of morality, and in the last instance "realization of one humanity in the messianic age" (BR 33), in which all injustice will cease to exist (RV 25). Cohen's idea is that morality confronts us with the infinite task of realizing the moral law in the material world, and that if we conceive of God as creator and moral archetype and as grounding both the material world and the moral law (cf. Seeskin 1990 p. 103), as in traditional monotheism, we will see that God, as Being (*Sein*) sustains the world of becoming as *Dasein*, while he at the time guarantees the possibility of a harmony between nature and morality (cf. BR 50 f.):

> Die Idee Gottes bedeutet die Gewähr, dass immerdar Dasein sein werde für die unendliche Fortführung der Sittlichkeit. Ohne diese Gewähr bliebe die Ethik eine Theorie ohne deren notwendigen Abschluss, den der Hinweis auf ihre unendliche Praxis bilden muss. Mit der Gottesidee gewinnt […] (die Ethik) erst ihren Abschluss. […] Gott […] bleibt ein […] Grundbegriff, allerdings nicht für den Beginn der Fundamentierung, sondern allein für ihre Vollendung; aber diese Vollendung könnte ohne ihn nicht erfolgen (BR 51, cf. also BR 60).

This clearly corresponds to Kant's conception, according to which ethics does not need religion as its basis, but that morality inevitably leads to religion and the idea of a "moral law-giver", to which he connects the idea of a "final end for the creation of the world" ("Endzweck der Weltschöpfung") which at the same time is the "final end of man" ("Endzweck des Menschen") (cf. Kant: Rel., Vorrede). – As a continuation of this idea we find then in Cohen the conception of a "messianic" hope for the realization of a "kingdom of morality" as a "kingdom of ends", or "one humanity in the messianic age" (BR 33). Closely releted to this "messianic" conception we also find in Cohen's thought the idea of an "ethical socialism" (cf. concerning this Cassirer 1996 and Launay 1992 p. 89, 95 and 98; see also below p. 52 ff.).

It is important to see how the aforementioned ideas presuppose religion as their origin and for their genesis.

> Der "messianische Idealismus" entsteht unter Mitwirkung der Vernunft, nicht der wissenschaftlichen Philosophie, weil es dieser nicht gelungen ist, die "übersinnliche Wirklichkeit der Zukunft" sicherzustellen. Das hat erst der "religiöse Gedanke" der profetischen Vernunft geleistet (Holzhey 2000 p. 56; cf. RV 340 f.).

"Messianic" ideas are present and are of great importance also in several other German-Jewish thinkers during the 20th century, as W. Benjamin, E. Bloch and T. Adorno, and also in the late philosophy of M. Horkheimer. Characteristic for Cohen's messianic thinking is that his primary concern is the confidence ("Zuversicht") in the "future of mankind" (BR 33), which, in contradistinction to the ideas of e. g. Adorno, Bloch and Benjamin, is not conceived in apocalyptic terms and as a break with history, but as a progress in humanity within this world: "[…] ein Jenseits zur Vergangenheit und Gegenwart der geschichtlichen Erfahrung an der Entwicklung der Völker […] im Unterschiede vom eschatologischen, ist der klare Sinn der messianischen Zukunft" (RV 340). – Against an "immanent messianism" of this kind, as we could perhaps designate it, one could, I think, reasonably object that it cannot sufficiently account for the injustice and suffering of past generations. And we see the relevance of M. Horkheimer's remarks in this respect, when he points out that a complete justice never could be realized within history, "denn selbst wenn eine bessere Gesellschaft die gegenwärtige Unordnung abgelöst und sich entfaltet haben wird, ist vergangene Elend nicht gutgemacht und die Not in der umgebenden Natur nicht aufgehoben" (Horkheimer 1970 a p. 69).[22]

Horkheimer does not however concede anything stronger than the possibility of "(eine) auf Sehnsucht gründeten Theologie", or at most a "theological postulate" (cf. Horkheimer 1970 p. 81). And, he asserts, because of our knowledge of evil in the world we cannot claim with any certainty that there is a good and almighty God: "[…] dann kann man sich also auch nicht auf Gott berufen. Man kann nur handeln mit dem inneren Antrieb, möge es so sein [...]" (ibid.).[23]

Cohen characterizes, however, the idea of God that is relevant in this regard and the idea of the "messianic God" in the "correlation" to "humanity" (cf. BR 60) as "the God of ethics" (cf. BR 64 and 77, and RV 23 f.): This idea of God, Cohen asserts, is "replanted" from monotheistic religion to ethics (RV 25), and does not represent really and strictly speaking, the "God of religion" (cf. RV 23 f.). In this respect we have to admit that this first line of argumenta-

---

22 Cf. also A. Wellmer's remarks on Adorno in this regard: "[…] an der Wahrheit […] müssten auch die längst Gestorbenen noch teilhaben, die Versöhnung der Menschen unter einander müsste auch die Toten noch einbeziehen. Dies aber lässt sich, wie Adorno sehr wohl wusste, nur noch theologisch denken. […] Gericht, Erlösung und Auferstehung sind Kategorien eines radikalen Bruchs mit der geschichtlichen Welt; dies gerade macht sie zu theologischen Kategorien" (Wellmer 1986 p. 94 f.).
23 Concerning these issues, see e. g. Schulte 1994 and Brumlik 1994; cf. also Wiesner 1986 p. 45 ff. For a survey of the main ideas of Cohen's messianism, see Poma 1997, chapter. 11.

tion leads from ethics to religion and its legitimacy only in a restricted sense. The, in a true sense, *religious* concept of God (cf. BR 64) we will according to Cohen apprehend first as we turn our attention to the further two lines of argumentation in his Kantian philosophy of religion. These have in common that they both concern a question regarding "a new concept of the human being" (cf. BR 57) in terms of what we could characterize as the irreducible individuality or subjectivity of the human individual (cf. Launay 1992 p. 90 and 93), or as in Cohen's formulation: "the complete sense of individuality of the human being" ("die volle Individualitätsbedeutung des Menschen") (BR 60), and which is one of fundamental concerns of Cohen in his late philosophy, in connection with the *religious* idea of God as the "God of the individual" (BR 65) in "correlation with the human individual being" (BR 67; cf. also BR 77, and RV 25). And it is in virtue of these concepts as the point of departure it seems adequate to talk about a transformation of Kantian philosophy of religion by Cohen.

3. Compassion (Mitleid) and the complementation of ethics by a religious consciousness

One of the lines of argumentation in Cohen with regard to the limitations of a merely ethical standpoint and of the ethical universal concept of the human being (cf. BR 52 ff.), and which according to Cohen leads from ethics to religion, builds on ideas that are absent in Kant's philosophy of religion, and represents, on the contrary, an explicit critique of Kant from Cohen's side. According to Cohen, we are, from a purely Kantian-ethical attitude, not able to come to an adequate understanding of the Other in his/her "concrete individualization" (BR 87); i.e. of other persons as genuine individuals, because a purely ethical point of view in terms of respect for others as ends in themselves only can allow for an understanding of other persons as general "instances" ("Beispiele") of humanity. I can, Cohen claims, only meet the Other as a genuine or "concrete" individual through an attitude of compassion (Mitleid), which emerges by my experience of him/her as a suffering human being.

The "ethical" concept of the human being

Cohen understands, as mentioned above, ethics as a doctrine of the human being; it depends on a "foundation" ("Grundlegung") of the human being or of "an idea of the human being" (cf. BR 52), i.e. in terms of a normative self-knowledge of the human being (cf. Holzhey 1993 p. 24f.). Ethics constitutes in virtue of this the central core of the contents of philosophy (ERW, Einleitung; see also Winter 1994 (1980) p. 312).

According to Cohen's interpretation of Kant in his "Kants Begründung der Ethik" it is not the first formula of the categorical imperative ("the logical principle" of the universalizability of my maxims) which constitutes the core of Kant's ethics. This core lies in "the teleological principle" of the humanity in every person as an end in himself,[24] and, next, in the idea of every rational being's will as a universal law-giving will and the concept of a kingdom of ends as a community of autonomous beings or as a "systematical con-

---

24 This is stressed also in ERW: "Handle so, dass Du Deine Person, wie die Person eines jeden Andern jederzeit als Zweck, niemals bloss als Mittel brauchst. In diesen Worten ist der tiefste und mächtigste Sinn des kategorischen Imperativs ausgesprochen; sie enthalten das sittliche Programm der neuen Zeit und aller Zukunft der Weltgeschichte" (ERW 303 f.).

nection of different rational beings through common objective laws" (Kant: Grl. 433). It is according to Cohen's understanding of Kant in these teleological moments that "the authentic contents of the formal moral law" could be adequately grasped, i.e. such that the foundation for the claims of a universal legislation is constituted by the idea of a universal community of autonomous ends in themselves. The community of autonomous beings implies essentially "die Aufeinanderbezogenheit sich in ihren Handlungsmaximen, also in ihren Gesetzgebungen, als Endzwecke anerkennender vernünftiger Wesen" (Winter 1994 (1980) p. 332). And a maxim or a "law of action" that can be universalized is then a maxim which implies the recognition of all other human beings as ends in themselves (cf. on this Winter 1994 (1980)).

Even if the question of the most adequate interpretation of Kant's ethics in this respect will not be an object for consideration here, in my opinion Cohen's understanding of Kant's ethics in this regard, i.e. according to which the "teleological" concept of human beings as ends in themselves becomes the basic concept in relation to the concept of the universalization of maxims, is the right one. Against J. Ebbinghaus' explicit criticism of Cohen's alleged "distortion" in his interpretation of the categorical imperative, where Cohen according to Ebbinghaus disregards how Kant introduces the concept of the human being as an end in himself as "a necessary consequence of the law", and therefore, illegitimately, transforms the categorical imperative into "ein Gesetz eines Endzweckes" (Ebbinghaus 1994 (1956) p. 156), there are strong reasons to assert that a reading of Kant's argumentation in Grundlegung II, like Cohen's, is the most adequate (cf. on this Bonaunet 1993 p. 153 ff. and p. 190 ff.).[25]

---

25 Cohen's interpretation here anticipates some of the most influential interpretations among recent moral philosophers and Kant-scholars, such as e.g. A. Donagan and A. Wood (see Donagan 1977 p. 233 and Wood 1999 chapt. 4).

The Kantian concept of the human being as an end in himself and as a member of a "kingdom of ends" as a "united humanity" forms the basis also for Cohen's own ethics. He elaborates his ethics in ERW, but some of the basic features are presented also in BR og RV. The following brief sketch is mainly built on these two works. – The human being cannot adequately be understood only as an individual in itself, nor as belonging only to the family, one's social class or nation. Man ought at the same time, first, to be understood in terms of his belonging to a state, as citizen. While the individual as belonging to the family and so forth, according to Cohen's terminology, is an "instance of a plurality" ("Mehrheit"), as a citizen one is raised towards a "universality" ("Allheit"), through which one is brought closer to a true self-knowledge: "Er soll sein isoliertes Individuum abstreifen lernen und sein wahres Selbst in der Allheit finden, die der Staat ihm erschliesst" (BR 52). The development of a true I-identity, which begins through the stages of "plurality" in family and society, and is continued by integration in the "universality" of the state, is at this stage, according to Cohen, still incomplete: The "universality" which is granted to the human being as a citizen is still an incomplete "universality", – a complete universality is fulfilled only insofar as the human being becomes a "citizen of humanity" ("ein Staatsbürger der Menschheit") (ibid.). But the state and one's citizenship in a state constitutes according to Cohen's conception an indispensable stage of transition and a mediation between the merely individual human being as an "empirical individual", and the idea of the universal humanity (Menschheit) (cf. RV 16). But anyway: "Alle Hoheit, alle Wahrhaftigkeit verleiht nur die Menschheit dem Menschen, der ohne sie in aller seiner sinnlichen Realität nur ein Schattenbild wäre" (BR 52). It is, in other words, "the universal humanity" of the human being that gives the human person his or her human personality (cf. BR 53).

By raising himself towards this "universality of humanity" the human being delivers himself from the egoism of the individual and from all the "dangers of self-love and self-righteousness" (cf. ibid.). And it is "the humanity in one's person" to which the human being subjects himself as he subjects himself to the "moral law" (BR 52). In this way we see that the "respect for the moral law" in reality is a "respect for humanity" (cf. BR 102), as respect for the ethical dignity of every human being (BR 79). The universal "humanity" of the human being, in virtue of which it is "Selbstzweck" and "Endzweck", is according to Cohen's conception connected with the universal ethical character of rationality which belongs to the human being.[26]

Cohen asserts, however, that there is a fundamental limitation inherent in this concept of the human being of ethics, i.e. in the ethical concept of the human being in terms of the universality of the human being (BR 52). Politics and ethics both strive towards defeating egoism and individualism. But this defeating of an egoistical individualism ought not to imply an abandoning of the indi-

---

[26] E. Winter objects against both Cohen and Kant that the principle of the dignity of the human being as grounded on this universal ethical character of rationality (Vernunftnatur) in the last instance must be admitted to be based on an, in its turn, not justifiable decision ("Entscheidung") (cf. Winter 1994 (1980) p. 332). Even if this problem cannot be discussed here, in my opinion it is possible on the basis of material in Kant's ethical writings to make a reconstruction of a justification of the claim of respect for every human being as an end in himself. Kant's concept of the "humanity" of the human being may be exposed in terms of its rational nature as an end-setting and value-constituting being, and as, in virtue of this, belonging to an order distinct from the "order of values" merely, i.e. as the order of values which is constituted in virtue of the existence of endsetting beings, as themselves forming an "order of *dignities*" – Important elements for an interpretation in these terms are found e.g. in some works of C. Korsgaard (see e.g. Korsgaard, 1996 chapter 4), and A. Wood (see Wood 1999, chapter 4). But we find the basic idea already in R. Otto, who characterizes the human being as an end in itself in terms of "die allen Wert begründende Würde" (cf. Otto 1981 (1931)). (Concerning this cf. also Bonaunet 1993 p. 220 ff.).

vidual. "Der Ethik aber ist kein anderes Mittel gegen das Individuum gegeben als die Allheit, die Erhebung des Individuums zu ihr und seine Auflösung in sie" (BR 55). And therefore:

> Es eröffnet sich [...] die wichtige Einsicht: dass der Begriff des Menschen keineswegs allseitig durch die Ethik bestimmt wird dadurch, dass das Individuum in die Allheit des Staates und des Staatenbunds der Menschheit aufgehoben wird. [...] wenn auch das Individuum schliesslich in die Allheit sich aufheben muss, so muss es doch in der Allheit Individuum bleiben; zwar ein solches der Allheit, nicht des Egoismus (BR 56).

The human person ought not to be, quite simply, "dissoluted" in universal humanity (cf. BR 57). Accordingly, the (concept of) the individual must be articulated, or, as expressed in Cohen's terminology, "produced" or "zur Erzeugung kommen" (BR 56).

Cohen's criticism of the shortcomings and limitations of the Kantian ethics, which at the same time must be regarded as a criticism of his own Kantian conception of ethics, implies in other words that ethics with its basic concept of respect for every human being in himself, in virtue of his universal humanity and ethical character of rationality (moralische Vernunftnatur), does not sufficiently take care of the existence and the claims of the concrete-individual being. The sense in which Cohen claims that this is the case will be explained in the broader presentation of his thinking on these matters below.

Already the "relative communities" (of the family, nation and so on) "take the human being back from universality" (Allheit), and refer it again to the "pluralities" (Mehrheiten) one belongs to. And in order to sustain his or her striving towards universality the human being also needs, as Cohen expresses his point, a "passage" through such "pluralities". In other words, Cohen points out how the social contexts man belongs to on the one hand support the formation of his identity, while they at the same time also contribute to a mediation of the particularity of our social existence with the ethical universality, i. e. of the universal humanity (cf. e. g. BR 60 f.).

But anyway, this is not in Cohen's opinion sufficient to provide the framework for an account of the human "concrete individuality" and "uniqueness" (Einzigkeit) of the human individual for which Cohen is searching in his late philosophy.

Cohen's critique of the limitation of Kantian ethics concerning its account of the unique individuality of the human being anticipates a line of criticisism that has been raised against Kantian ethics also by our contemporaries. Recently, S. Benhabib has formulated some critical points concerning the resources and possibilities of any ethical position within the Kantian tradition, from Kant himself to J. Rawls and J. Habermas, of representing the perspective of the "concrete Other" as distinguished from the merely "generalized other": While the standpoint of the "generalized other", focusing on the norms of "formal equality and reciprocity" in terms of respect, duty and dignity, abstracts from the "individuality and concrete identity of the other", a genuine turning towards the other as the "concrete Other" implies that "I confirm not only your humanity but your human individuality". And this becomes possible only in virtue of moral feelings of "love, care, sympathy and solidarity" (cf. Benhabib 1992 p. 158 ff., and also 1986 p. 340 ff.).[27] And Habermas

---

27 We also find a formulation of this kind of criticism in A. Honneth's contribution to the "Cambridge Companion to Habermas". Honneth claims that there is a need of transcending the conceptual horizons of Kantian ethics in order to award greater theoretical attention to "the uniqueness of the individual person" (Honneth 1995 p. 307), which must be an "essential core of every theory of morality" (ibid. p. 290). This concern represents a challenge for modern theories of morality in the Kantian tradition (ibid. p. 291), which "all too frequently have [...] denied" this perspective its proper place (cf. ibid. p. 319). Honneth characterizes this problem in terms of a "conflict" (p. 291 and 315), an "opposition", a "confrontation" or at least as a "productive" but "irresolvable" "tension" (p. 309 and 319) in relation to a Kantian ethics. (See also T. Mc Carthy's answer and partial defence of the Kantian position in this respect in his review of the "Cambridge Companion" in Ethics 1997.)

himself also has been grappling with some of the same problems, conceding that the self as conceived in terms of discourse-ethics as a member of an unlimited community of discourse, "unveils itself in every individual [...] as something universal after all" (Habermas: 1998 p. 161; see also below p. 92 ff.).

What is mostly interesting for us now is to look more closely into how Cohen anticipates these problems and philosophically thematizes the problem of the "concrete individual". There are in Cohen's late philosophy two ways or routes leading to a recognition of the concrete human individual. One leads via the concept of "compassion" (Mitleid) to the *"concrete Other"*; a second way leads via the concepts of guilt and forgiveness to what we can designate as the *"concrete I"*. Cohen's thinking on these matters is, I think, interesting not only with regard to the problem of a complementation of the Kantian concept of the human being in his "humanity", as emerging from a center within the Kantian tradition itself, and in virtue of its relevance for the actual contemporary discussion concerning the concept of the "concrete Other". Cohen's thinking revolves around and seeks to clarify phenomena such as compassion and guilt/forgiveness, which are in themselves important moments of a philosophical understanding of the human being.

We should note here that Cohen explicitly states that his intention is to provide a philosophical articulation of the *concreteness* of the individual. Not only as U. Hommes remarks:

> [...] der Rückgang auf die konkrete Faktizität des menschliches Daseins (wird) von Cohen selbst ganz ausdrücklich mit dem Hinweis darauf begründet, dass der Mensch "als sittliches Vernunftwesen [...] nur eine Abstraktion" ist (U. Hommes, here after Holzhey 1994 p. 18).

But, further, Cohen also speaks directly on how he "den Menschenbegriff *lebendig und konkret* zu machen hat", i.e. by focussing on the "lonely, isolated human soul" in its suffering (BR 93). And he contrasts the "concrete individualization" (*"konkrete Individualisierung"*) that is implied in the (religious) love towards the human being, against the *eros* of art, which is "(eine) erzeugende Liebe des Gefühls, die sich dem Menschen selber erzeugt, nicht aber *ihn sich gegeben sein lässt*. Dahingegen liebt die Religion den Menschen an dem Erkennungszeichen seines Leides" (BR 87). Cohen also characterizes this contrast by saying that: "Die reine Liebe der Kunst hat in ihrer Produktivitätskraft ohnehin wenig Ähnlichkeit mit dem leidenschaftlichen Drang, der *sich dem Individuum hingibt*" (ibid.) (all ital. KB). – I understand this as meaning that Cohen presupposes an encounter with the Other, in his/her "concrete individualization". And the Other, to whom I "devote" ("hingeben") myself, and his suffering, cannot, as far as I can see, be conceived in terms of a pure "production", as "Erschaffen", "Erzeugen" or "Hervorbringung". I think it must be admitted that there exists here a moment of "givenness". And I think the same would apply also with respect to my own guilt in relation to myself as an "absolute individual". And I therefore have problems with following K. Seeskin when he seems to sharply oppose Cohen's approach in terms of "rational construction" against Buber's conception of an "immediate encounter" (cf. Seeskin 2001 p. 182).

On the other hand, I can't see that admitting these points with respect to Cohen, would imply any commitment to an interpretation of Cohen's thought as a position which amounts to a transition from transcendental philosophy to existentialism, and thus to Rosenzweig's reading of Cohen as an existentialist. It is, in my opinion, sufficient to admit that we find rudiments or onsets ("Ansätze") towards a "philosophy of dialogue" in Cohen's late philosophy, as he moves the "center of gravity" towards existential questions (cf. Ollig, 1978 p. 362 and 369f., 1979 p. and 1979a p. 350), and in this sense, a "turn towards the concrete human being" (cf. Holzhey 1994 p. 18). But this does not imply the assertion that Cohen abandons his transcendental philosophical ground conception (cf. Ollig 1979a p. 336). First we will now concentrate on the problems of compassion (Mitleid) and the "concrete Other".

The discovery of the "thou" and the necessity of transcending ethics

Above we have suggested how there are, according to Cohen, certain shortcomings in the ethical "doctrine of the human being", with the concept of the human being as articulated by ethics and, as Cohen expresses himself, in the "deepest depth" of the ethical concept of the human being (cf. RV 15): The ethical abstraction implies that something is lacking with regard to the full individuality of the human individual. In a certain regard this ethical abstraction is legitimate and necessary for a correct self-understanding on behalf of man: Through ethics the "I of the human being" becomes an "I of humanity". And by this the human being is raised out of and above his egoistic isolation: *Humanity* is what gives the human being its true individuality (cf. RV 16). But in another sense, then, ethics is, according to Cohen, not able to adequately grasp the human being in his or her individuality: "Die Ethik kann den Menschen schlechterdings nur als Menschheit erkennen und anerkennen. Auch als Individuum kann er nur der Träger der Menschheit sein" (RV 15).

Already from a theoretical perspective I can acknowledge that there exist different individuals of all different kinds, and so also human individuals, even if I through "thinking", according to Cohen, the "Platonist"[28], cannot grasp singular objects: Through thinking we can only grasp an object as something universal. This applies also for my "ethical thinking", which correspondingly cannot grasp the individual human being as such (cf. BR 76 and 86). In virtue of ethical reason, I recognize that every human being ought to be respected as "Selbstzweck" and "Endzweck", but that means as belonging to and as an "instance" ("Beispiel") of a universal humanity. So the ethical recognition in terms of universal respect, as grounded in

---

28 Concerning Cohen's Platonic background, see e. g. Schulthess 1993. Cf. also Wiehl 2000 p. 409 ff.

ethical "thinking", does not then by itself enable me to understand the Other in his or her "concrete" and "unique" individuality.

Cohen in RV approaches this problem by saying that: "Neben dem Ich erhebt sich, und zwar im Unterschiede vom Es, der Er". This in itself does not however presuppose any transcending of the horizon of ethics. The other as "He" (Er) can still reasonably be understood as an another "instance" ("Beispiel") of the humanity we both belong to. But further, I also meet the Other as *"thou"*. And Cohen now poses the question if I really have an adequate understanding of the Other as *thou* only in virtue of my understanding of him as another I – on the same level as myself – within humanity as a "universality" (Allheit), or, in other words, by my understanding of myself and the Other as of equal dignity insofar as I understand that "ich bin einer von allen" (cf. E. Tugendhat (1984 p. 162)). Cohen suggests that we need a special "discovery of the thou", and that perhaps "erst das Du, die Entdeckung des Du mich selbst auch zum Bewusstsein meines Ich, zur sittlichen Erkenntnis meines Ich zu bringen vermöchte". But could this still belong to the competence of ethics, i. e. "to bring to discovery the thou", "wenn doch ihr Zielpunkt nur die Allheit ist, welche in der Menschheit allein sich erfüllt?" (RV 17).

The question of the limited competence of ethics becomes, Cohen says, urgent when we are confronted with the problem of the *thou*, – "wenn [...] (diese Frage) noch bei dem (Problem) des Er verschleiert bleiben mochte" (RV 17).[29] And Cohen's standpoint soon becomes clear: "Das Du bringt ein neues Problem in den Begriff des Menschen [...]" (RV 18). And the Other, whom I adress as *thou*, requires another concept of the human individual, which the discovery of the thou reveals (cf. ibid.), and which transcends the concept of the human being's universal "humanity" and of the individual as an "instance of humanity", as this is established by ethics.

---

29   "Das Er ist mit einer Neutralität behaftet, die es nur schwer vom Es unterscheidet" (RV 18f).

Cohen emphasizes however that we still essentially have to understand this thou as a thou within "humanity": "das Du gehört jedoch der unendlichen Gliedreihe der Menschheit an", or it belongs to the "unity of humanity". There ought to be no "suspension" ("Aufhebung") of the ethical concept of the human being. The concern is about a "complementation" ("Ergänzung") of the concept of the human being of ethics, because ethics falls short facing "the new problem of the thou" (RV 18), insofar as this *thou* demands a concept of the individual which ethics, from its own basic presuppositions, is not able to account for.[30] But according to Cohen "the new concept of the human being", i. e. as a concept which constitutes a complementation of the concept of the human being as established by ethics ought to have a continuity or "homogenity" with the ethical concept. It is essentially a matter of "eine Ergänzung als Fortsetzung" (BR 58). And this means that with regard to the concept of the "concrete Other", the ethical fundamental concept of respect for the ethical dignity ("Würde") of every human being, remains an indispensable basis.[31]

---

30 According to A. Poma, Cohen's occupation with the human being in his "concrete individualization" (BR 87) is a consequence of a critique from the Marburg theologian W. Hermann, but in part also P. Natorp, who claimed that Cohen's Kantian ethics did not afford to the *individual* his or her appropriate place (cf. Poma 1996 p. 24 f.).

31 Cohen's articulation of the concept of the "thou" constitutes I think an important background for the further elaborations of this concept and of the problem of the "concrete Other" in the thinking of M. Buber and E. Levinas. Buber, who formulates his philosophy of the "thou" in his "I and Thou", published in 1923, however explicitly denies having been influenced by Cohen concerning this matter, in spite of his public disputes and *Auseinandersetzung* with Cohen on other problems, such as the question of zionism, during the second decade of the 20. century. – The relations between the positions of Cohen and Levinas is explored to some extent by R. Gibbs (1992, chapter 1 and 8), K. Huyzing (1995) and, most detailed, by E. Wyschogrod (1980). For an extensive discussion of the relation between the po-

The fact of suffering within human existence

The point of departure for Cohen's account of the concept of the "concrete Other" is the fact of suffering within our human existence ("die Tatsache des allgemeinen Menschenleids" (BR 70)). The fact of suffering opens a new understanding of the human being in his individual existence: "es liegt schon eine positive Aufklärung über den Sinn des individuellen Menschenlebens in dem Satze: an der Erde Brust sind wir zum Leide da" (BR 54).[32] I experience my own suffering, but not only my own; I also see the suffering of the Other (cf. BR 54 and RV 19 f.).

It is an ethical task to make man's existence on earth better, and therefore to lessen human suffering (cf. RV 21). Thus suffering is not an indifferent matter for ethics, nor is ethics indifferent facing suffering, – ethics with its recognition of the dignity of the human being in his humanity. Our moral tasks are indisputably in connection with "the sensible conditions" of the human being (RV 19). But even if ethics implies a claim of lessening the suffering of humanity, its concern with regard to suffering is, according to Cohen, insufficient: The ethical obligation to lessen suffering does not take seriously enough the central importance of suffering within the human existence, and does not answer the practical [33] questions the recognition of the Other's (or my own) suffering implies.

---

sitions of Cohen, Buber and Levinas, see Seeskin 2001. – A treatment of this question would however be far beyond the scope of this essay.

32 Cf. also RV 19 f.: "'Die Träne quillt, die Erde hat mich wieder'. So bezeichnet auch Faust durch das Zeugnis der Träne den Menschen in seinem Erdendasein", and RV 170: "Willst du wissen, was der Mensch sei, so erkenne sein Leiden".

33 – in contrast to the metaphysical *theoretical* interest for for instance the essence and origin of suffering (cf. RV 20 ff.).

> Im Leiden geht mir plötzlich und unaufhaltsam ein grelles Licht auf über die Flecken an der Sonne des Lebens. [...] Es ist der ganze Sinn der Ethik, als der Lehre vom Menschen und vom Menschenwerte, an dem ich verzweifeln muss, wenn dieser Menschenwert sich vorzugsweise im Leiden ausmünzt. Der Sinn der Menschheit wird mir hinfällig [...] (RV 21).

"So stellt uns diese Einsicht vom Leiden vor die schwerste Alternative der Ethik" (RV 22); the concept of the human being which ethics establishes seems here, Cohen asserts, to have reached its limit.

But what, then, is it concerning human suffering and especially the suffering of the Other, which leads us beyond the concept of the human being of ethics? We cannot here immediately answer this question. For this purpose it is necessary to follow Cohen through certain reflections, first concerning human suffering, and further, concerning some insights he will extract from the "sources of Judaism".

Human suffering is not identical with physical pain, even if suffering is not completely separated from the physical: "suffering is also pain" (RV 157). But the suffering of the human being is not the same as the pain of the animal. For the human being, physical pain is raised to the level of the psychological (cf. also BR 90), "und somit in die gesamte Komplikation des Seelischen" (RV 157). Therefore, suffering becomes "eine prävalierende Tatsache des Bewusstseins, als eine das ganze menschliche Bewusstsein erfüllende und alle anderen Vorgänge und Tätigkeiten desselben mitbestimmende" (ibid.).

Human suffering appears in many forms, and of course through sickness and death (cf. BR 80). It is, however, the social suffering of poverty that is the primary focus for Cohen's attention. For Cohen poverty is the essence of the social misery of the human being. And: "das allgemeine Menschenleid (wird) am sozialen Kriterium der Armut erfasst" (BR 72). Of what use would it be, Cohen asks, if all sickness and death were brought to an end, but not poverty; "würde dadurch nicht nur das menschliche Elend durch Verewigung gesteigert?" (ibid.).

But how should I practically act in confronting suffering? First, absolutely not as according to stoicism, – nor as following Spinoza, who (also) in this respect is a stoic. Stoicism has, Cohen asserts, no understanding of the importance of suffering in the human existence, insofar as suffering here is declared to be an *adiaforon*. One question concerns whether my own suffering ought or can be indifferent for me; according to Cohen this already constitutes a serious problem with regard to stoicism's understanding of this matter. But in any case, even if a human being strives to ignore his own woe and well-being, and succeeds in this, "so dürfte er doch über das Wehe des Andern nicht hinwegsehen, wenn etwa selbst über sein Wohl" (RV 153).

For Cohen there is an asymmetry with regard to how I should act in relation to my own suffering, unlike in relation to the suffering of the Other. For now, we have to concentrate on Cohen's conception of how I ought to act in relation to the suffering of the Other.[34] And facing the suffering of the Other, I am never allowed to be indifferent (cf. RV 19). This is true in relation to physical evil, even if my own physical well-being and woe could remain indifferent to me (RV 155). And above all, an attitude of indifference in relation to the suffering of the other becomes wrong if it concerns social inequalities and the suffering of the poor. "So wird ihnen gegenüber die Gleichgültigkeit zu einer Unwahrhaftigkeit […], ja zu einer Grausamkeit" (RV 153). Overcoming indifference towards the suffering of the Other is already an ethical obligation (cf. above). Cohen asserts that from the point of view of an ethics of social responsibility, stoicism appears as either "hypocrisy" or "unforgivable ignorance" (cf. ibid.).

---

34 The question of how I should act in relation to my own suffering Cohen discusses both in BR and RV in connection with the questions of guilt, punishment and forgiveness (see below p. 73 ff.).

Besides his criticism of the attitude of indifference of stoicism in relation to the suffering in human existence, Cohen rejects as absolutely inadequate, and again, particularly in relation to the suffering of the poor, a standpoint of seeing this as something he deserves, as punishment for his guilt, and of accounting for the misery of the Other in terms of his bad state of character and moral quality (cf. BR 72). It is not true that the virtuous and guiltless get their rewards by wealth and riches, while the guilty get the punishments they might deserve by poverty. If this were the case we ought to regard the wealthy one as guiltless, the wealthy one "der vielmehr als Inhaber und Verüber der Gewalt gebrandmarkt werden muss" (BR 73). There is no connection or correspondance between social and moral differences: "[…] der Gerechte, und ihm geht es übel; der Schlechte, und ihm ergeht es wohl!" (RV 152, cf. also 264 f.). Further, if I would consider suffering as punishment for guilt, this would also imply claiming for myself the power of watching all social misery from the view of an omniscient "judge of the world" (BR 72). And finally, any understanding like this would be in contradiction to a basic ethical attitude. Because: "wie sollte ein solches Individuum zur Allheit sich erheben können, wenn ihm aller Sinn für Gleichheit und Gerechtigkeit verstopft ist […]?" (ibid.) In short: Any attempt to measure or compare the inner value or dignity of a human being "mit dem äusseren Scheine seines Erdenloses (ist) eitel und nichtig, kurzsichtig und verblendet" (RV 26).

The Jewish prophets and "the discovery of the fellow human being"

Cohen's practical-philosophical thinking is sustained by an ethical socialism. This is clearly expressed in his view of poverty as the fundamental suffering of humankind. At the same time we find, both in BR and RV, clear examples of how he means to be able to ground his ethical socialism in Jewish prophetism: It is the prophets who, in accordance with their "social politics" first recognize poverty as the real suffering of man, as "das eigentliche Menschenleid" (BR 73). And, likewise, it is the prophets who first realize how the presence of poverty cannot be understood as (deserved) punishment for sin: The poor is innocent and suffers without being guilty (cf. BR 74).[35] "Das Leiden ist nicht Strafe; sonst wäre Armut Strafe, und Reichtum Tugend und Tugendpreis. Hingegen ist vielmehr die Armut das Wahrzeichen der Frömmigkeit" (ibid.).[36]

Before he turns to an interpretation of certain features of prophetism (to which we will return below), Cohen discusses in RV the concepts of "the stranger" and "the noachid" as these are found in rabbinism and the Talmud, and which he asserts have had decisive influence with regard to the genesis of the ethical universalistic reason, through the formation of the concept of "the fellow human being" ("der Mitmensch", i.e. the human being "with" whom I am existing). Cohen cites the possibility of a ("natural" and "historical") experience of the human being as an "element in a series", "ein Mensch neben Menschen, ein Nebenmensch" (RV 132), i.e. a hu-

---

[35] Cohen would then dismiss as inadequate what M. Nussbaum designates as "the judgment of *nondesert* (this person did not bring this suffering on himself or herself)" (Nussbaum 2001 p. 321) and takes as a necessary cognitive element of compassion (cf. ibid. p. 311 ff.). – L. Blum's conception in this regard comes at least closer to Cohen's: "[…] that the object has in some way brought the suffering on himself or deserved it, […] such ways of regarding the object do not necessarily undermine compassion, and they are not incompatible with it. […] it is possible (and not necessarily unwarranted) to feel compassion and concern for him, simply because he is suffering" (Blum 1980 p. 512).

[36] Cohen points out how the Hebrew language gives guidance towards this insight: "poor" originally means "depressed" ("bedrückt"), and this at the same time also means "humble" ("demütig"). "Demut ist aber die Tugend des Armen, das Kennzeichen des echten Menschenleids. Diese Bedeutung lässt sich aber auch in dem hebräischen Worte für fromm erkennen. So werden die Armen zu den Frommen und die Frommen zu den Armen" (BR 74).

man being "beside" me. This, however, in no way constitutes any complete concept of the human being: "Es ist [...] notwendig, dass eine begriffliche Erkenntnis eintrete, welche [...] (eine) Ergänzung zum Nebenmenschen liefern muss" (RV 132). The experiences of the others as "human beings beside me", as "Nebenmenschen", are "crossed" ("durchkreuzen") by "the claims of my fellow human being" (RV 133). It is the concept of the human being as a moral rational being of ethics which brings us beyond the experience of the other as "Nebenmensch", and towards understanding her/him as "Mitmensch".[37] And it is first within the perspective of ethics we are able to see how our fellow human being is leveled down to a "human being beside me" merely or "ein Nebenmensch", even if as we will see below, according to Cohen, ethics in itself can not give us any complete understanding of the Other as a fellow human being (cf. RV 133).

When it comes to the genesis of the concept of "the fellow human being" Cohen emphasizes the development from the (political (RV 142)) concept of "the stranger" ("der Fremdling"/"der Fremdling-Beisass" (the stranger who lives in the country and who ought to have his "share in the law of the country", because "the law has to be uniform for all") (cf. RV 140f.)) from "the first beginnings of biblical monotheism", to the (ethical (RV 142)) concept of "the noachid" ("the son of Noah") which is elaborated in rabbinism (Talmud): God by his covenant with Noah places himself in "correlation" with nature and with humanity, with all human beings, everyone as created in the image of God, and therefore being brothers. "So ist denn schon nach diesem Bunde Gottes mit Noah jeder Mensch der Bruder des anderen" (RV 136). And by this the equality between human beings is grounded, the equality which turns all

---

37 "Die Menschheit offenbart [...] im Nebenmenschen erst den Mitmenschen" (BR 53).

human beings into "fellow human beings" ("Mitmenschen) (cf. RV 135 ff.).

In other words, by this there is established a mutual relation or a "correlation" human being – human being, or more exactly: *Mitmensch – Mitmensch*, which at the same time in a certain sense constitutes a basis for the "correlation" human being – God, that is the fundamental axis or "fundamental equation" (RV 132) of all true religion.[38] The concept of "the noachid", again, becomes in its turn the ethical ground of the political rights of the stranger: "Der Mensch ist dem Menschen nicht ein Fremder, der auch ein Sklave sein könnte [...]" (BR 76). The stranger can, without having to profess a faith in the God of monotheism, join the Israelite state, under the condition of his acknowledgment, as an ethical rational being, of certain fundamental ethical obligations (such as to abstain from blasphemy, murder, robbery and incest [...]) (cf. RV 143).

For their genesis, the concepts of "universal humanity" and of "the fellow human being", according to Cohen, presuppose monotheism. Only monotheism can constitute humanity, the concept of "one universal humanity", in relation to one God (cf. RV 173, see on this Cassirer 1996 (1935) p. 101 ff.). And it is also from the conception of the one God that "the stranger" appears as a "fellow human being" or *Mitmensch* (cf. RV 144). We are here, however, talking of insights which a philosophical ethics in its turn is able to reconstruct and justify. For Cohen, as for Kant, ethics does not presuppose religion for establishing its validity. Ethics has its "selfsubsistence" in relation to religion, while religion, even if it, according

---

38 "Die Korrelation von Mensch und Gott kann [...] nicht in Vollzug treten, wenn nicht vorerst an der eingeschlossenen Korrelation von Mensch und Mensch. Die Korrelation von Mensch und Gott ist in erster Linie die vom Menschen, als Mitmenschen, zu Gott [...]" (RV 133). – A detailed examination of the place of the concept of "correlation" in Cohen's philosophy is found in Xie 1996.

to Cohen's conception in his late philosophy, no longer can be "dissoluted" in ethics, does not possess any "selfsubsistence", but only a "peculiarity" in relation to ethics.

In light of the preceding considerations, Cohen next turns his attention to some fundamental concerns of Jewish prophetism. On the one hand, the essence of the message of prophetism can be seen in the realization of one humanity in relation to one God, in the messianic age (BR 32). But on the other hand, prophetism also focuses on human suffering, and primarily on the poor as the suffering one:

> Die soziale Unterscheidung von arm und reich bildet die schwerste Frage an den Begriff des Menschen, an die Einheit und Gleichheit der Menschen. Der *Nebenmensch* wird unvermeidlich zu einem *Gegenmensch*, denn die soziale Differenzierung erscheint nicht als eine [...] Nebenordnung, sondern als Unterordnung, Unterwerfung, so dass dawider das Problem des *Mitmenschen* sich erheben muss (RV 148; ital. KB).

In relation to the suffering human being, and still especially to the suffering poor, the question of the constitution of the Other as *Mitmensch* is then posed again, and in a more radical way than ethics can do. For, Cohen asserts, ethical respect has in itself "no eye for whether the human being is poor and miserable, or wealthy and rich" (BR 79). What is really required is a keen eye for the social differences and the suffering of the poor.

On the basis of this, Cohen's criticism of stoicism now also becomes sharpened: The fellow human being cannot come to my consciousness if its woe and well-being remains indifferent for me. Such indifference becomes an obstacle for the formation of the notion of the fellow man (cf. RV 154). "Und es entsteht die Frage, ob nicht gerade durch die Beachtung des Leidens bei dem Anderen dieser Andere aus dem Er in das Du sich verwandelt" (RV 19).

Compassion and recognition of the "concrete Other"

This brings us now finally to the core of Cohen's concept of the "concrete Other" and the foundation for a complete concept of "the fellow human being". The point of departure is constituted by the experience of human suffering and the insight of suffering as "the essence of the human being" (RV 170), and according to Cohen, above all poverty as the big suffering of humankind (cf. RV 156) and as the fundamental obstacle for the "brotherly equality" of all human beings. For through poverty, not only is the fellow human being leveled down to a being "beside" me, as *Nebenmensch*: The concept of the fellow human being, and even also of the Other as *Nebenmensch*, becomes here a contradiction, insofar as the poor one rather becomes *Untermensch*, i.e. a being *below* me (cf. RV 170). But now, by the experience of the suffering of the Other "regt sich zugleich ein heftiges Gefühl der Beziehung": The suffering of the Other becomes not the object for any theoretical experience: "es verwandelt sich in einen Affekt. […] So entsteht das Mitleid" (BR 76).

And through compassion (Mitleid) I will now see the Other, no longer as a "human being who stands against me" or "below me" or only "beside me" (as "Gegenmensch" or "Untermensch" or "Nebenmensch"), nor only as an "instance" ("Beispiel") of humanity: I recognize the Other as a fellow human being ("Mitmensch") in the full sense of the word, as a concrete individual who is of immediate concern to me: "So entsteht hier […] in dem Affekt des Mitleids […] erst das Individuum als solches […]", "geht das Individuum als solches hervor" (BR 83). "Das Mitleid wird wachgerufen, als die neue Urform der Menschlichkeit. […] Der Mensch beginnt im Mitleid den Menschen zu lieben, den Nebenmenschen zu verwandeln in den Mitmenschen" (RV 169, cf. also 164 f.). Along with this discovery of the fellow human being out of the experience of suffering (cf. RV 159) belongs, then, also the discovery of the Other as a "concrete individual", – "(eine) Entdeckung des Individuums am leidenden Menschen" (BR 94), "an seinem Leiden mit meinem Mitleid" (BR 88).

The concrete individuality of the human being thus, according to Cohen, reveals itself through the human suffering; the Other appears to me as a human individual whom I can "grasp" ("erfassen") in his suffering, through my compassion (Mitleid) (cf. BR 85). The subject of our compassion is, as Cohen says, "das lebendige Wesen der menschlichen Seele, der Mensch, nicht als ein Typus, nicht als ein Begriff, weder der Mehrheit noch der Allheit, sondern eben das Individuum" (BR 80). We are grasping the Other as given to us in his "absonderliche [...] Besonderheit" or "naked isolation", "which transforms itself to individuality" (BR 87). Thus compassion or *Mitleid*, "das Mitleid des Menschen am Menschen" (RV 169), awakens the recognition of the individual and our understanding of the human being's "entire significance of individuality" ("die volle Individualitätsbedeutung"), within the universal humanity (BR 60).

Regarding the genesis of the concept of "universal humanity", Cohen also asserts that the genesis of the notion of the one, concrete individual human being is connected with monotheism: To the one God there corresponds one humanity, but at the same time the concept of the one human being as a "unique individual" ("einziges Individuum") (BR), corresponds to the idea of the one, unique ("einzige") God (cf. Rosenzweig 1994 (1924) p. 141).

Compassion, however, constitutes no immediate and naturally present "motivation" ("Regung") within our human consciousness according to Cohen. Foundational to compassion, philanthropy and charity ("Mitleid", "Menschenliebe" and "Nächstenliebe") is first the theoretical knowledge, that I am not able to know myself as an I unless I know myself as related to another I: A relation must be present, "theoretisch des einen Ich zum anderen Ich" (BR 76). And further, as we already have seen above, we must acknowledge the presupposition of ethical respect for every human being as a representative of universal humanity. Compassion, philanthropy, and charity have their roots in ethical respect: "Von ihr erst zweigt sich das Mitleid ab" (BR 80). Compassion (Mitleid) cannot then according to Cohen's conception – *versus* Schopenhauer – constitute the *foundation for ethics*,[39] but can only grow from ethics as its ground ("auf dem Boden der Ethik"), which means from respect for the universal humanity in every human being. When I see a human being suffering, not only will "the theoretical indifference disappear behind the ethical interest" (BR 76), but at the same time, we could say, ethical thought will give way to compassion as an ethical-religious feeling (Gefühl):

> Diese Frage greift ans Herz. Vom Herzen muss die Reaktion ausgehen, die Gegenwirkung, nach der wir suchen, damit der Mitmensch entstehen kann, [...] ein Gegenfühl [...] gegen das Leiden, das selbst nicht nur Erkenntnis bleiben darf, sondern kraftvolles Gefühl werden muss (RV 160).

"(So) wie theoretisch des einen Ich zum anderen" (cf. above), "so praktisch des eigenen Gefühls zu dem Leide (des Anderen)" (BR 76).

Through the experience of suffering – and above all, suffering as conditioned by social inequalities – the fellow human being is then brought fully to our "discovery" ("Entdeckung"), i.e. through the effect of suffering on our feeling of compassion (cf. RV 160). And even if this insight presupposes ethics, there is, Cohen asserts, "a big step" ("ein weiter Schritt") from ethical respect to compassion and love of the Other as a "unique individual" ("einziges Individuum").

Compassion, however, ought not to be understood as any passive reaction: *Mitleid* is "full", "entire" and "pure" *activity*, and constitutes according to Cohen an "affective factor" of the "pure" ethical will. Thus it can, in some sense, be considered as related to respect or *Achtung* as a "feeling of reason" ("Vernunftgefühl"), according to Kant, even if it contains further affective moments.

39 Concerning Cohen's critique of Schopenhauer, see BR 76, and RV 20, and 63 f.

It is as an "original power of the pure will" ("Urkraft des reinen Willens"), and, therefore, as a "fundamental power of the ethical universe" that compassion opens up for or constitutes the key to the fellow human being in his or her concrete existence (cf. RV 164). And it is because compassion constitutes an "original power" of our ethical will that the suffering of the Other implies an ethical *claim* on me: The suffering of the Other *ought* not to remain a matter of indifference to me. I feel "called to compassion" ("zur Mitleidenschaft aufgerufen"). "[…] er leidet, und ich sollte nicht wenigstens mit ihm leiden?" (BR 76 f.).

With the concept of "the fellow human being", from the experience of the suffering individual, emerges then a "new concept of the human being" (cf. above p. 37 and 48), and by "compassion" as "the concept of discovery" ("Entdeckungsbegriff") (RV 165). And compassion has thus become a kind of "original feeling" ("Urgefühl") in human beings, through which the human being is, as it were, "invented", – "den Mitmenschen und den Menchen überhaupt" (RV 166), as the concrete individual.

Cohen, however, expresses his wonder at this, that compassion is a kind of "original feeling" (RV 166), and has become one of the most common affects of the life of the soul of the human being (cf. BR 76), because compassion according to Cohen, as we remarked above, does not constitute any immediate natural "motivation" ("Regung") and a "matter of course" in human beings. In BR he characterizes this as a paradox, that I shall have compassion with and love of the Other: "Wurm, der ich bin, von Leidenschaften zerfressen, der Selbstsucht zum Köder hingeworfen, soll ich dennoch den Menschen lieben" (BR 82). In RV he talks about this as an "enigma" ("wie ein Rätsel"): "Wie kann der selbstsüchtige Mensch einen andern lieben […] ?" (RV 170, cf. also 518). Cohen reflects here Kant's wonder at the "moral predisposition" of the human being and its "incomprehensibility" (cf. Kant: Rel. B 57 f.).

A preliminary assessment

Now, what insights have we gained from the preceding presentation of Cohen's concepts, if any? At least Cohen has made a contribution to a philosophical articulation of some features of our human self-understanding. It represents perhaps – in any case partly – more a piece of "Existenzerhellung" (K. Jaspers) (cf. Kamlah 1973 p. 15) than an argumentative philosophy. Or it might be that Rosenzweig's sympathetical characterization of Cohen is the most adequate one. According to this it is a basic feature of Cohen in his thinking that he doesn't as much really "prove" ("beweist"), "auch kaum je aufweist, sondern immer nur denkt" (Rosenzweig 1994 (1924) s. 138).

Cohen's insights ought reasonably to be accepted as constituting an important complementation of a rationalistic ethics in terms of universal respect. His endeavours can be read as an attempt to achieve a balanced mediation between a Kantian ethics of reason and an ethics of compassion, or between *Vernunftethik* and *Mitleidsethik*, and, I think, as a reasonable proposal for a solution of the controversies concerning the place of reason and compassion in philosophical ethics since its beginnings in ancient Greece. While Cohen rejects and does not accept any pure ethics of compassion or sympathy, he at the same time emphasizes the ethical importance of compassion, as a needed complement to respect: Everyone who recognizes that there exist differences in our human existence, moral and social, and doesn't make the fallacy of considering these as identical, "der wird Mitleid achten und ehren und hegen als ein notwendiges Grundmittel in der sittlichen Entwicklung des menschlichen Bewusstseins" (BR 76).

Defending *Mitleid* or compassion as an indispensable component of a complete moral consciousness is a concern which Cohen shares also with other philosophers of the 20th century, especially M. Scheler. And Cohen and Scheler seem to arrive – from their different philosophical perspectives, Kantianism and phenomenology

– to conceptions that are in certain respects basically in agreement with each other. According to Scheler "Mitgefühl" is a foundation for love ("Liebe"). And the individual person and his/her value as an individual becomes a fact or "comes to givenness" for us at all only through and in an act of "Liebe" (Scheler: Wesen [...] p. 168):

> das Wesen einer fremden Individualität, das unbeschreiblich ist und im Begreifen nie aufgeht ("individuum ineffabile") tritt nur in der Liebe oder im Sehen durch sie hindurch ganz und rein hervor. Ist die Liebe weg, so tritt an die Stelle des "Individuums" sofort die "soziale Person" [...] (ibid. p. 163).

Corresponding to how Cohen emphasizes the necessity of universal respect of the human being as an "instance" of humanity as a presupposition and basis for "Mitleid" and "Menschenliebe", Scheler also asserts that "die Liebe zum individuellen Personzentrum eines jeden [...] setzt die Liebe zum Exemplar "Mensch" voraus" (ibid. p. 110).

There are, however, differences between the conceptions of Cohen and Scheler, but these are, I think, of minor importance, and do not disrupt the fundamental agreement between their visions. 1) Scheler characterizes "Mitgefühl" (which contains "Mitleid" together with "Mitfreude") as a "reactive factor", while only "Liebe" implies an "act of spontaneity" or an active "movement" (cf. Scheler: Wesen [...] p. 78 and p. 147). On the contrary, Cohen considers "Mitleid" and "Menschenliebe" as essentially the same (cf. BR 76: "Das Mitleid verklärt sich zur Menschenliebe"), and attributes a character of spontaneity already to "Mitleid" (cf. above). – But also according to Scheler there exists a mutual foundational relation between "Mitgefühl" and "Liebe" (cf. Wesen [...] p. 107 ff. and p. 147 f.), which implies a close connection between them. 2) Scheler distinguishes between three levels: "Mitgefühl", general "Menschenliebe" (Humanitas) and ("acosmistic") "Personliebe". But *humanitas* which concerns every human being as "Exemplar des Menschen" (cf. ibid. p. 110) could in some respects be said to correspond to Cohen's *"re-*

spect" "(Achtung)". To Scheler's "Personliebe" corresponds, then, Cohen's "Mitleid"/"Menschenliebe". 3) When Scheler at one place (ibid. p. 149) rejects attempts to deduce "Liebe" from "Mitleiden" and "(ein) erbärmliches Gefühl einer Liebe zu den Leidenden als Leidenden", because anything like this constitutes a "highly doubtful basic fact", this could be read as a direct criticism of Cohen. But also for Cohen, as we have seen, *Mitleid* does not constitute any primitive-original feeling within human nature. 4) On the other hand there seems to be between Cohen and Scheler – with respect to their philosophy of religion – a very interesting agreement, insofar as Cohen understands "Mitleid"/"Menschenliebe" as a "religious" feeling, such that it is only through "Mitleid" one attains to the consciousness of God as the one who protects the suffering (cf. Scholz 1922 p. 279), while at the same time also the love of God becomes manifested in "Mitleid", and Scheler correspondingly asserts, first, that "pure sympathy" constitutes a foundation for or a "reference" towards the acceptance of a theistic "Metaphysik des Weltgrundes" (Wesen [...] p. 77, cf. also p. 136), and, further, connects (the "acosmistic") love of persons (Personliebe) to charity or neighbor love (cf. ibid. p. 136) and understands this as an *amare in Deo*, as "(ein) Mitvollzug (von) [...] (Gottes) Liebe zur Welt" (ibid. p. 166). In addition, Scheler says concerning "the general love of human beings" ("allgemeine Menschenliebe") that it is a essential presupposition for the love of God, while it at the same time is "experienced" and "thought" on the basis of God's love of human beings (Liebe Gottes zum Menschen) (ibid. p. 111). This leads us now to a more difficult problem with regard to the understanding of Cohen's concerns.

Compassion and the problem of transcending ethics

According to Cohen's conception there is, as we have seen above, a correspondence between the "correlation" between human beings as "unique" ("einzige") individuals and a "correlation" between a human being as "unique" and the "unique" ("einzige") God of monotheism, i. e. as a God who is not only *one*, but at the same time essentially "unique" ("einzig"), because God is "Being" ("Sein"), and therefore distinguished from all that is merely "existing" ("Dasein") (cf. above p. 29 ff.). In connection with this idea, Cohen asserts that an attitude of compassion (Mitleid), which implies recognition of the Other in his/her genuine individuality, belongs to a distinctive *religious* consciousness: "Was der Vernunft in der Ethik nicht gelingt, die allgemeine Menschenliebe, das bringt sie in der Religion zustande" (RV 167). "[…] erst die Religion in ihrer Eigenart, d.h. die Korrelation von Mensch und Gott (hat) den Mitmenschen erzeugt" (RV 187; cf. also BR 98).

The necessity of making this step from ethics to religion is, however, hardly immediately evident. First, Cohen's claim that a Kantian ethics of reason lacks the capacity to grasp the human individual, might be disputed (cf. McCarthy 1997). It might be asserted, as Cohen himself pointed out in ERW, that the "humanity" formula of the categorical imperative implies the requirement that "der Zweck concreter und lebendiger und persönlicher in jeglichem Menschenantlitze bewährt und verwirklicht werden müsse" (ERW 304). Still, we might admit that compassion constitutes an emotional complement of respect of universal humanity, which seems to require a larger degree of detachment, and as implying an accentuation of the individuality of the Other in relation to the recognition of every human being as an end in him-/herself in virtue of possessing a common rational nature.[40] But, second, even if we grant this point to

---

40 It might be objected that it is unclear why just suffering reveals the unique individuality of the Other, in contradistinction to respect in Kant's sense,

Cohen, it is not easy to see any decisive reasons for the standpoint that including compassion in the ethical consciousness, and correspondingly: recognizing the Other as a genuine individual, presupposes our transcending of a merely philosophical-anthropological horizon, and a transition to, according to Cohen, a peculiar *religious* attitude. P. Natorp remarks in this connection that: "(es ist) gar nicht einzusehen, dass die Ethik das Individuum überspringen müsse" (Natorp (a comment on BR) p. 116). On the other hand, J. Habermas most recently has suggested a position that seems to come very close to Cohen's in this regard, conceding that: "devotion to the suffering other [...] comes up short within an intersubjectively conceived morality of justice" (Habermas/Mendieta 2002 p. 164), while at the same time indicating that "the unconditioned right of each creature not to be overlooked, to be acknowledged for what it is" is preserved in the religious conception of "the essential core of the fully individuated other [...] marked as having been made 'in the image of

---

since also suffering, like humanity is a general property. I think however that this objection misses the moment of emotional intensity or strength of compassion (cf. Blum 1980 p. 509 and 512 f.) which is provoked by the suffering of the Other, as just this suffering individual. As H. Arendt observes about compassion, as a *passion*: "Its strength hinges on the strength of the passion itself, which in contrast to reason, can comprehend only the particular, but has [...] no capacity for generalization" (Arendt 1963 p. 80). Compassion is then, by "its very nature" (ibid.) directed "toward specific suffering" and is focussed on "persons in their singularity" and "the reality of persons in particular" (ibid. p. 85). No longer having this focus, it would turn into a mere "sentiment", "depersonalizing" the suffering, and lacking the ethical power belonging to both compassion and principles of reason (cf. ibid. p. 80 ff.). L. Blum also distinguishes compassion from other altruistic emotions or attitudes, which are not, as compassion is, "directed to particular persons", but "to classes of persons [...] or to general conditions" (Blum 1980 p. 508).

God'" (ibid. p. 158). In what follows I will now examine more closely Cohen's assertion that a complementation of the ethical obligation of universal respect, through compassion towards "concrete individuals" requires a transition to a religious attitude, and the question of whether and in what sense this claim might be redeemed.

A basic methodological principle in Cohen's philosophy of religion with regard to a justification of religion on the basis of ethics, and of religion in its "peculiarity" (cf. e.g. BR 16f. and RV 18f.) in relation to ethics, consists in investigating whether there are insights that are essential for an adequate self-understanding of our human ethical existence, – having their origin and genesis in (monotheistic) religion, which means for Cohen primarily Judaism, that ethics as a philosophical discipline itself is not able to integrate within its own limits.[41] Philosophical ethics is, as we have seen above, according to Cohen able to account for and justify the principle of the fundamental equality and dignity of all human beings and the moral claim of universal respect for human beings as ends in themselves, and so to appropriate this principle as its own, even if this concept of the equal dignity and unity of all human beings has its historical *origin* in the idea of the *one* God, as creator of *one* humanity (cf. RV 138, 144f. and 173; cf. also ERW 55 and 214).[42]

---

41   Cf. BR 43: "Nun müssen wir aber fragen, [...] ob in der Tat die Ethik in der Verfassung ist, alle Probleme zu behandeln, die hergebrachterweise in der Religion entstehen, und von denen angenommen werden darf, dass ihr Fortbestand berechtigt und gesichert sei[...]."
42   Thus it is, at best, not subtle enough if one asserts that "Cohen deduces love of neighbour as a basic concept of his ethics from the Jewish religion", and that e.g. the commandment of non-killing for Cohen has its validity in virtue of its being a Divine commandment, while E. Levinas, as distinguished from Cohen, does well without "theological premisses", and anchors this commandment in "phenomenological intuitions" and an "anthropocentrical philosophy" (cf. Levy 1997 p. 136ff.), and that Cohen's ethics, unlike Levinas' "autonomous" ethics, in the last instance is "heteronomous" (cf. ibid. p. 143).

Compassion or *Mitleid*, as the attitude through which I discover the Other as a human fellow being or *Mitmensch*, and as *thou* in his/her "concrete individuality" has according to Cohen this same historical origin, i.e. within the context of monotheistic religion, but as we have explained above, in connection with the ideas of God not only as one, but as "unique" ("einzig"), and of each human being as unique in virtue of its correlation to God as its creator. It is, Cohen points out, the Israelite prophets who first formulate the principle of compassion towards the suffering individual, and, as we have seen, according to Cohen's reading of the prophets, above all the poor one, who is in a special way the subject of God's love (cf. BR 72 ff., and RV 26 f.). And in Cohen's view, the relation between fellow human beings constitutes a "lower correlation", which can only exist as an "inner constituent" of a "higher correlation" between God and the human being (cf. RV 133, 153 f., 169, 264 and 405).

– A similar view comes to expression by R. Horwitz, by the way referring to Z. Levy: "While for Cohen a social sin is a sin against God, for Levinas social sins must not be expressed theologically" (Horwitz 2000 p. 182). But neither Levy nor Horwitz takes sufficiently account of Cohen's basic thought of the selfsubsistence of ethics in relation to religion. This fundamental thought in Cohen is clearly explicated e.g. in BR 120 f.: "[…] da die Autonomie […] durch die Ethik sichergestellt ist, und mit ihr der ethische Begriff der Idee der Menschheit, so können die Gebote Gottes nur als Hinweisungen und Anleitungen zur Autonomie gewürdigt werden". And an ethical action "folgt nicht aus einem fremden Beweggrunde, noch auf einen fremden Befehl. Sie ist der Erfolg des Willens, dem Autonomie zusteht" (RV 190). Concerning Cohen's thesis of the independence of ethics in relation to religion, see also (e.g.) RV 141 and 393. Further, Cohen does not link the distinctive character of religion to the apprehension of the moral law as the commandment of God (as does Kant (see KPV A 233; MdS. 443 and 487)). The essence and peculiarity of religion is, according to Cohen, found in other factors.

There is something significant in Cohen's conception of Judaism, and especially the proclamations of the Israelitic prophets, as an "epoch-making turn" (BR 75) and as the origin of the thought of the importance of compassion with the "concrete Other". The consciousness of the compassion with individual persons is at least in no way prominent, neither in classical Greek nor in Hellenistic thinking. For both Plato and Aristotle it is the universal, and therefore also the universal aspect of the human being that is the focus of their attention (cf. e.g. Vlastos 1973). And the stoics, who attain to the moral insight of a universal respect for human beings as rational beings, neglect, as Cohen with indignation complains of (as we have seen above p. 51 f. and 56), the understanding of the ethical relevance of human suffering.

Further we can concede a point to Cohen insofar as religion is a place where the value of the individual and compassion towards the suffering is emphasized and encouraged as the right attitude. Cohen attributes in RV importance to religion just in this regard: God has, by his commandments, "awakened" or "originated" ("gestiftet") in us compassion for the poor (cf. RV 183); God's love of the human being, as an individual, is an "archetype" ("Urbild") for our task of loving the fellow human being (our *Mitmensch*), and God teaches us by this to "create" the human being as the fellow human being: "So muss Gott zum zweiten Male Schöpfer werden, indem er den Menschen als Mitmenschen durch den Menschen selbst, durch den Vernunftanteil der Religion zu erschaffen lehrt" (RV 170).

The difficulty of understanding Cohen's thinking in this respect is connected to his assertion of the presence here of a peculiar content, which cannot be preserved if we attempt to take it away from its original religious context. This is because his idea that the understanding of the Other as my fellow human being in the full sense of the word and as a "concrete individual" essentially is connected with a correlation between God and the human individual (cf. Wyschogrod 1980 p. 48). Or in other words: The Other can be recognized in his/her full individuality only on the basis of a preceding and concomitant, religiously apprehended correlation between God and the human being (cf. RV 131 ff.; see also Levy 1997 p. 190).

Cohen, as we have seen above, already has opened up and claimed the possibility of a philosophical – ethical formulation and justification of the principle of universal neighbour love in terms of respect for the equality of every human being as an end in himself (cf. above p. 38 ff. and 66). But in what sense ought we, then, to admit that compassion or *Mitleid* as directed towards the "concrete individuals", distinguished from respect for human beings in virtue of their common humanity, resists what we could term an immanent philosophical articulation and justification?

One thing that religion (monotheistic Judaism) originally provided was the "emotional basis" (cf. Schmid 1995 p. 308) for the principle of compassion. And Cohen's claim of legitimizing religion in its "peculiarity" in relation to ethics could then at least be accepted in the sense of his highlighting the historical importance of religion with regard to generating a more complete moral consciousness, – a feature which Kant also acknowledges with respect to Christianity (cf. SF, VII, 44).[43] At the same time, Cohen could also be said to show the rationality of religion by pointing out its "share in reason" insofar as compassion is a characteristic affect of religion (cf. BR 79) and the contents of religion in this respect are in accord with

---

43   Cf. also Habermas' concession in this regard: "So glaube ich nicht, dass wir als Europäer Begriffe wie Moralität und Sittlichkeit, Person und Individualität, Freiheit und Emazipation […] ernstlich verstehen können, ohne uns die Substanz des heilsgeschichtlichen Denkens jüdisch-christlicher Herkunft anzueignen" (Habermas 1988 p. 23). See also, Øfsti 2000 p. 273 ff. and p. 295.

the requirements of a complete moral consciousness, and insofar as religion still is a place where compassion toward our fellow human beings, especially the poor and oppressed, is "awakened" and sustained.

"Homogenity" with ethics is an incontestable negative criterion for the legitimacy and rationality or "share in reason" of (a) religion *überhaupt* (cf. Ricken 1992 p. 192 f. and Haeffner 1997 p. 195).[44]

However, this will apply already and in the same way also with regard to the principle of the equal worth of all human being, in virtue of their belonging to one universal humanity, as created by the one God, and of respect for everyone as an "instance" of this humanity. *Mitleid*, then, does not seem to be in any unique position. Cohen's claim about the principle of *Mitleid* concerning the "concrete individual" – as distinguished from universal respect of human beings – requiring a transition from ethics to religion proper can hardly be said to be redeemed.

Like Kant (cf. e. g. Rel. B iii), Cohen asserts that ethics, independent of religion, can account for the "humanity" of the human being. But we should also note that he occasionally refers to compassion as "die neue Urform der Menschlichkeit" (RV 169; cf. also BR 98) and as something that gradually has become one of the "most natural affects in the entire life of the human soul" (BR 76). By this he indicates that compassion could be understood within a philosophical-anthropological framework. On the other hand, he firmly denies that an "anthropological ethics" could give an adequate account of compassion as "a concept of principle" (RV 20). Corre-

---

[44] Cf. also Schillebeeckx 1994 p. 59: "The criterion is [...] humanity. A religion which damages and destroys human beings and human dignity is a religion that denies itself. A religion which humiliates human beings is [...] a mistaken way of believing in God."

spondingly, he asserts the indispensability of a religious standpoint in this regard:

> [...] die Norm der ethischen Liebe [...] hat uns den Mitmenschen zur Entdeckung gebracht in der Liebe von Mensch zu Mensch; die Liebe Gottes hinwiederum hat in ihrer ethischen Norm das Mitleid zum Universalismus der Humanität ausgeweitet (RV 187).

His claim is not intended merely in the sense of a genealogy of morals. But ought we really to concede this point to him, and if so, in what sense?

Cohen has provided no decisive arguments against the possibility of a philosophical – anthropological articulation and justification of the attitude of compassion as far as I can see. On the other hand, only a successfully completed philosophical – anthropological explication of compassion as a basic ethical attitude would provide a definitive rejection of his scepticism in this respect. And if we accept this as a premise, we could, insofar as no such account exists, acknowledge a core of truth in Cohen's conception. On the relation between philosophy and religion, J. Habermas contends that: "Philosophy [...] will be able neither to replace nor to repress religion as long as religious language is the bearer of a semantic content that is inspiring and even indispensable" and which "eludes [...] the explanatory force of philosophical language and continues to resist translation into reasoning discourses" (Habermas: 1998 p. 51).

Habermas also asserts that in fact "indispensable potentials for meaning *are* preserved in religious language, potentials that philosophy has not yet fully exhausted" nor "yet translated into the language of [...] presumptively generally convincing reasons" (Habermas/Mendieta 2002 p. 162; ital. KB). One example in this respect concerns precisely the "devotion to the suffering other" (ibid. p. 164; cf. also above p. 65), and "the concept of the individual person, which the religious language of monotheistic doctrine has indeed articulated from the very beginning with all the precision one could wish for", in contrast to the "deficit [...] of philosophical attempts at translation" (ibid. p. 162). For in this respect "the basic concepts of philosophical ethics, as they have developed up to this point, [...] fail to capture all the intuitions that have already found a more nuanced expression in the language of the Bible" (ibid.).

This concession does not however, as Habermas also points out, imply any assertion of the inherent impossibility of a philosophical "translation" and justification of the value of the attitude of compassion and the recognition of the individual person or the concrete Other. In terms of this we will then have to reject Cohen's claim of a *necessary* transition from ethics to religion, if his position should be interpreted as implying this (as I think it should), while we might accept his claim if we understand this in a weaker sense.

However, beyond this line of argument, according to which in Cohen's conception the concept of the fellow human being or our *Mitmensch* presupposes a specific context of religion to be fully apprehended, there remains also another route from ethics to religion, connected with another question. And, Cohen says, "In der Lösung dieser Frage aber erst vollzieht sich die Eigenart der Religion bestimmter und deutlicher als beim Mitmenschen" (RV 193).

4. Moral guilt as problem of a Kantian philosophy of religion

On guilt as a problem of ethics

The third and last line of argumentation in Cohen's Kantian philosophy of religion consists in a continuation of certain problems from Kant's Religion innerhalb der Grenzen der blossen Vernunft. Cohen rejects the thought of a "radical evil" in human beings (see below p. 82 ff.), but his questions and discussions concerning recognition of moral guilt and redemption from guilt are very closely connected with Kant's treatments of the problems of the possibility of moral regeneration and forgiveness of moral guilt.[45]

The problems concerning the experience of failing in our strivings for moral autonomy, i.e. the problems of moral guilt and of the possibilities of redemption from guilt and a new beginning, were matters of considerable interest and subject to relatively extensive discussions within German philosophy during the first decades of the twentieth century, as in N. Hartmann (cf. Hartmann's Ethik, 1926, (especially chapter. 78)), M. Scheler (Vom Ewigen im Menschen, 1920), and above all in H. Cohen's late philosophy. In the thought of Cohen, the possibility and necessity of liberation from guilt turns out to be the most important basis for a transition from ethics to religion, and correspondingly, his most interesting argument for the legitimacy of participating in the practices and institutions of religion.

According to Cohen, the knowledge of moral guilt or "sin" belongs to our deepest human self-knowledge. As he states already in ERW: "es darf nicht verkannt werden, dass in dem Begriffe der Sünde

---

45 Concerning these problems in Kant's philosophy of religion, see Wimmer 1990 § 15.

der sittliche Begriff des Menschen vertieft und genauer zur Erkenntnis gebracht werden sollte, als es dem Altertum durch den Begriff der Tugend gelungen zu sein schien" (ERW 272).

These concepts of sin and guilt have their origin within a religious context where the moral claims are recognized as Divine commands (RV 236). But insofar as ethics with its claim of respect for human beings as ends in themselves (cf. above) can be separated from its origin in religion and be granted autonomy in relation to religion, because the fundamental moral claims can be grounded in an autonomous ethical reason, the concepts of sin and moral guilt as connected with transgressions of these claims, can be understood as *ethical* concepts. According to Cohen, recognition of moral responsibility and guilt already transcends ethics in a narrow sense: Ethics attributes to the human being a free, autonomous will, but only as a "pure will", as a will to the good. The recognition of a freedom of the will as a capability of choosing evil *or* good (cf. ERW 283), does not, Cohen asserts, belong to the foundation (Grundlegung) of ethics in a strict sense, but presupposes an articulation of human self-knowledge or an "experience of the human being" which belongs to a wider context (cf. RV 211 f.). Accordingly, the recognition of guilt does not belong to "the ethics of the pure will", as such, but it is in light of the claims of ethics that the human being acknowledges his guilt (cf. BR 53). Thus, we can designate this guilt as a moral guilt. Ethics cannot, then, reject the question of guilt or sin; it is, as Cohen asserts, "an ethical concept" (ERW 356) and "ethically legitimate" (BR 62), and must be sustained as "a fundamental ethical question for man" (RV 194; cf. also BR 65 f.).

Self-knowledge of guilt is closely related to a human being's knowledge of his/her moral responsibility: Insight into the freedom and moral accountability of the human individual already implies insight into individual guilt for moral failures. And *vice versa*: In the self-knowledge of moral guilt, the individual is constituted or consolidated as a moral subject and a free responsible person (RV 23;

BR 62). Cohen seems to attribute a special significance to our self-knowledge of transgressing moral claims, for our knowledge of our moral accountability and the idea of freedom as the basis for human action, as the only idea by which I can understand myself as an acting person (cf. Kant: Grl. 448). His claim is not that consciousness of moral responsibility is dependent on self-knowledge of guilt, but that guilt-consciousness reveals our responsibility in a special way.[46] At the same time, this recognition uncovers, in a radical sense, my irreducible individuality: *Ego sum qui feci*; it is *my* responsibility (cf. Ricoeur 1992 (1967) p. 229). As Cohen says: In the self-knowledge of sin and moral guilt "the individual [...] alone has to stand up for himself" and as, in his moral responsibility, "related exclusively to himself". Man here comes to know himself as a "living human individual", and as "an absolute individual" (RV 192 f.). "[...] dürfen andere die Urheber seiner Handlungen [...] sein? [...] Er muss sich also isoliert denken, sofern er sich sündhaft denkt. [...] die Einsamkeit kommt jetzt über ihn aus der Erkenntnis seiner ihn vor sich selbst isolierenden Sünde" (BR 62, cf. also 68). And every human being must ascribe to himself "uniqueness" ("Einzigkeit") (BR 62).

This becomes accentuated in the explicit confession of guilt wherein the recognition of guilt is expressed: "Wenn das Individuum sich als den Urheber seiner Schuld erkennen muss, so muss es sich auch als solchen bekennen. In diesem Bekenntnis erst kommt das Ich an der Tag" (RV 228). – Correspondingly, guilt is a phenomenon that essentially is uncovered in a first person's perspective (cf.

---

46 Cf. also P. Ricoeur who in accordance with Cohen's insights emphasizes how freedom amd moral guilt are components of a complex network, together with moral obligation (Ricoeur 1992 (1967) p. 229 f.): "[...] to affirm freedom is to take upon oneself the origin of evil. [...] Evil has the meaning of evil because it is the work of freedom." And: "if freedom qualified evil as a doing, evil is that which reveals freedom. By this I mean to say, evil is a privileged occasion for becoming aware of freedom." – See also Honnefelder 1975 p. 41.

Jaspers 1963 p. 23; cf. also ibid. (e.g.) p. 17 and 42), and through the self-knowledge of the acting subject (cf. RV 22 and 194).

Cohen is certainly not blind to the fact that, with respect to our concrete actions, we never are in possession of any absolute certainty concerning their degree of freedom and, accordingly, their moral quality, insofar as they represent a synthesis of freedom and necessity (cf. Rahner 1976 p. 104). We are agents situated also in a social world, and realize ourselves as free subjects in situations which are already historically and intersubjectively determined. These situations are in part characterized by the "objectivated results" of actions by others and "objectivation of the guilt of others" (ibid. p. 113 f.).

> Wir sind die, die unentrinnbar unsere eigene Freiheit subjekthaft in einer Situation vollziehen müssen, die durch Schuldobjektivationen mitbestimmt ist, und zwar so, dass diese Mitbestimmtheit zu unserer Situation bleibend und unentrinnbar gehört (ibid.).

Cohen himself points out that:

> Der soziologische Standpunkt verfolgt mit Bedacht und Recht den Grund der sittlichen Schäden in den Gegensätzen und Reibungen der sozialen Verhältnisse. Die Sünde ist hier die soziale Sünde. Die einseitige religiöse und religiös determinierte sittliche Betrachtung isoliert den Menschen in seiner sittlichen Kraft, und glaubt ihn durch diese Isolierung zum Individuum zu machen. Beide Gesichtspunkte bedürfen der Verbindung miteinander [...] (RV 210).

That we in our guilt also may have others who are "accessories" does not, however, in any way imply the annulment of the insight of a freedom "worin jemand der Einmalige, Unvertretbare wird, der sich weder nach rückwärts noch nach vorwärts, noch in seine Umwelt gleichsam weganalysieren und so von sich selbst entlasten kann" (Rahner 1976 p. 118).

The concepts of sin and guilt have, as Cohen points out, their origin within a mythological – religious context. While the *mythological* consciousness does not yet understand the individual as the origin and source of his or her own sin, but only as one who inherits the guilt of ancestors (cf. RV 23 and BR 61; see also ERW 344 f.), the *religious* individual realizes his or her own responsibility. In Cohen's account of the progressive development within Jewish religion, it is Ezekiel who is especially credited the recognition of the importance and responsibility of the individual, and the "discovery" ("die Entdeckung") of the individual (BR 56):

> [...] wenn nun [...] die Religion in der Selbsterkenntnis des Menschen ihren tiefsten Grund hat, so steht Jecheskel unvermittelt neben Sokrates. Wie dieser theoretisch in der Selbsterkenntnis den Menschen und mit ihm die Ethik begründete, so Jecheskel die Religion in der Selbsterkenntnis des Menschen von seiner Sünde (RV 23).

Cohen emphasizes in this regard the statement of Ezekiel that "the soul commits sins", where "the soul" according to Cohen's reading represents "the person" and "the individual", and therefore the "entire human being" as "originator" ("Urheber") of his sin (RV 222, cf. also BR 61 and ERW 283 f. and 346). This discovery of the human being as an individual through the attribution of sin is according to Cohen "the source from which every development of religion flows" (RV 23), or the "birthplace of religion" (BR 54).

Moral guilt is something the individual human being only can impute to himself. This is a point which Cohen stresses already in ERW (349 ff.), stating that: "Immer muss das Selbst das Forum bleiben für die Frage der Schuld" (ERW 351) and that knowledge of guilt must be self-knowledge (ERW 356). With regard to the moral guilt of others I am, Cohen asserts, not allowed even to raise the issue. The Other ought to be the object of my respect and compassion. And in order that compassion for the Other shall arise it is, according to Cohen, necessary that I refuse to ask the question of his or her guilt, because this would be an obstacle for attaining this end (cf. RV 193 and BR 72).[47] – An absolute delimitation of imputation of moral guilt

---

47 Cf. note 35 above.

to a first person's perspective or the perspective of the subject (cf. ERW 356), as Cohen seems to assert, is however problematical. A concept that restricts imputation of moral guilt to a first person's perspective harmonizes with a proper Kantian spirit. For Kant, it is also a fundamental idea that the attribution of moral responsibility and guilt primarily ought to be restricted to a first person's perspective. This is in a certain sense a sympathetic aspect of Kant's ethics, at least in part motivated from an ideal of precaution with regard to judging others and the quality of their moral dispositions: "Es ist […] Tugendpflicht […], den Schleier der Menschenliebe nicht bloss durch Milderung unserer Urteile, sondern auch durch Verschweigung derselben über die Fehler anderer zu werfen" (Kant: MdS 466). But an idea which sets up an absolute asymmetry between first person perspective, on the one hand, and second and third person perspective on the other, is in certain respects problematical. For an attitude towards the Other that implies weaking the dimension of imputation of responsibility will at the same time imply also that I don't take fully seriously his/her status as a moral – rational agent. In other words, insofar as the possibility of imputation of moral guilt is essentially connected with attribution of responsibility and accountability at all, a principle of absolutely refraining from attributing moral guilt to others seems to be incompatible with a recognition of them as accountable persons. And mutual attribution of accountability and responsibility are, in the last instance, constitutive for genuinely interpersonal relationships (cf. concerning this Korsgaard 1996, chapter 7, especially p. 189, 196, 206 f., and 212).

N. Hartmann also emphasizes how the Other demands or is entitled to attribution of accountability: "[…] er sieht sich in seiner Menschenwürde verletzt, wenn ihm die Zurechnung seiner Taten versagt wird" (Hartmann: Ethik p. 730 f.).

> Rechne ich dem Anderen nicht zu, was im Bereich seiner Verantwortung liegt, so negiere ich damit [...] ihn selbst als sittliche Person. Nimmt mir jemand die Verantwortung ab, die ich trage, so vergeht er sich an meinem Grundwesen als Person [...] (ibid. p. 732).

This brings us now to a closer look at Hartmann's position as we believe that constructing the elements of a possible dialogue between Cohen and Hartmann could throw some light on the problems we are discussing.

N. Hartmann on consciousness of guilt

We find in N. Hartmann's analysis of moral consciousness an insight into the ethical importance of the concept of moral guilt which corresponds to Cohen's in certain respects. Hartmann points out how the phenomenon of guilt consciousness is closely related to the "phenomenon complex" (Hartmann: Ethik p. 740) or the "fact complex" (ibid. p. 742) of responsibility and accountability. A consciousness of responsibility accompanies every moral act, – "sie ist vor der Tat im Aufsichnehmen so gut wie nach der Tat im Tragen und Einstehen mit der Person". Guilt comes into existence with the morally wrong action ("Vergehen") and as a consequence of it (ibid. p. 740). Hartmann also emphasizes the importance of the consciousness of guilt to recognizing the human being's character of a being of freedom: The consciousness of guilt is a witness of the ethical self-determination of the human being of an entirely other weight than the ideas of responsibility and accountability in themselves.

> Hier spricht etwas Urwüchsiges, Unverfälschbares aus der Tiefe des Menschenwesens hervor unmittelbar zum sittlichen Bewusstsein [...]. Der metaphysische Sinn dieser Erscheinung [...] liegt in ihrer Bezogenheit auf reale Selbstbestimmung. Denn "Schuld" bedeutet Urheberschaft [...] der Person selbst. Darum ist Schuldbewusstsein eindeutig auf Selbstbestimmung der Person bezogen (ibid. p. 741).

More determinately, the consciousness of guilt is the consciousness of the person's or the individual's "character of origin" with respect to his or her actions, but together with the consciousness of their moral unworthiness ("Wertwidrigkeit") (cf. ibid.). Likewise Hartmann can further state that in the negative testimony the human being brings against himself in his "Wertwidrigkeit", and in his (properly understood) "will to guilt", "erhebt sich das tiefere metaphysische Wesen der Person mit seinem Anspruch auf Unverletzlichkeit" (ibid. p. 742).

Against the objection that consciousness of guilt is only an illusion, Hartmann asserts that consciousness of guilt reveals and depends on real guilt: The one who is conscious of guilt is also "really ethically guilty" ("real-ethisch schuldig") (ibid. p. 743). It is hardly Hartmann's intention to deny the possibility of false and ungrounded guilt-feeling. But not all consciousness of guilt is false. And not only the consciousness of guilt, but also "being guilty" ("Schuldigsein") is "highly real", – "ein höchst reales und real empfundenes" (ibid. p. 740). Consciousness of guilt and the corresponding attitude of remorse ("Reue") cannot then, according to Hartmann, be psychologically explained away. They are necessary and proper consequences of the recognition of the ethical unworthiness ("Unwert") of an action (cf. ibid. p. 741). In other words, moral guilt has, according to this concept, a "real", "objective" character and represents, as P. Ricoeur expresses, "an ontological dimension of existence" (cf. Ricoeur 1992 (1967) p. 227). It has a *sui-generis*-character and cannot be reduced in terms of Freudian psychological explanations (cf. Gaita 1996 p. 33). But again, the existence of "real guilt" and a corresponding "authentic guilt-feeling" does not exclude the difficulties of deciding in different concrete cases whether real moral guilt actually is present. As M. Buber points out, "authentic guilt-feeling" often can be inseparably intermingled with the problematic, the "neurotic", and the "ungrounded" (Buber 1965 p. 127).

According to Hartmann's analysis, the consciousness of guilt is a heavy burden for the moral individual:

> In diesem engeren Phänomen haben wir eine eigenartige Zuspitzung dessen, was auch in der Verantwortung schon steckt: der Belastung der Person und ihres Tragenmüssens. Greifbarer und elementarer ist es hier gegeben – zugleich auch unabweisbarer und unentrinnbarer (Ethik p. 740).

And I cannot disclaim this guilt. I must bear it for the sake of freedom. Disclaiming the guilt I have incurred implies, Hartmann asserts, disclaiming my status of an autonomous person. "Träger der Schuld ist ja eben die Person, und alle Entlastung von ihr hat nur Sinn als Entlastung der Person. […] Das entlastete Wesen ist dann nicht mehr das volle Menschenwesen, nicht mehr die vollwertige Person" (ibid. p. 742).

According to Hartmann's understanding, it is an ethical task to bear one's guilt:

> Hat man sie […] auf sich geladen, so kann man sie sich nicht nehmen lassen, ohne sich selbst zu negieren. Der Schuldige […] muss die Erlösung […] ablehnen. Die Bewahrung der Schuld ist ihm wertvoll, ungeachtet ihrer lastenden Schwere; sie bedeutet ihm die Erhaltung seiner Person, die Wahrung und Anerkennung seiner Freiheit. Mit der Schuld würde er […] sein Menschentum preisgeben (ibid. p. 352 f.).

At the same time this implies that in Hartmann's view human existence is a tragic existence, because

> (die Schuld) erhebt sich drohend gegen die eigene Person, fällt auf sie mit ihrer Last und drückt sie nieder. Ja, sie kann die Person moralisch erdrücken mit ihrem Gewicht, so dass sie sich nicht mehr aufzurichten vermag. Sie kann den Menschen zu Verzweiflung und Selbstpreisgabe führen. Denn die Tragkraft der Person ist begrenzt (ibid. p. 740, cf. also p. 818).

But precisely in this respect Cohen's view is different: He poses the question if guilt can be forgiven and redeemed. He poses this question because he sees that morality itself implies a claim of moral regeneration, that requires means against "moral despair". The morally responsible individual cannot allow himself never again to be "upright" (cf. Hartmann). At the same time the acquired moral guilt also seems to irreversibly belong to my existence (cf. Honnefelder 1975 p. 32). Thus the problem of redemption from moral guilt is generated, as a problem for ethics: Guilt is generated when I act against the claims of morality. It then appears to belong irreversibly to my existence, and seems insofar as it generates moral despair to make moral regeneration impossible. This regeneration, however, is itself a moral requirement as a claim of the same morality. We must search, therefore, for a solution of the problem of redemption or liberation from moral guilt.

The problem of the possibility of a moral regeneration – Kant and Cohen

There is, as we have seen above, an inner connectedness between the concepts of moral guilt, the moral subject or person, and freedom, that is constitutive for the ethical existence of the human being (cf. Honnefelder 1975 p. 41 and 45). At the same time, however, there seems to be a kind of antinomy between the individual's consciousness of his/her own guilt, insofar as this consciousness implies a simultaneous "moral despair" by the guilty individual, and the claim of a moral regeneration of the individual who is guilty.

In Kant's philosophy of religion there are some distinctive problems with regard to the possibility of a moral regeneration, because the point of departure for Kant's questions concerning the possibility – and necessity – of a moral regeneration is his doctrine of the "radical evil" of the human being. Man makes, in virtue of his free will and through a fundamental decision, a reversal of the relation between the moral requirements of the categorical imperative and his "self-love" such that our compliance with the moral claims is made dependent on that this does not imply any hindrance of the strivings of our "self-love", – instead of inversely: to restrain our "self-love" in accordance with and out of the requirements of morality. Regardless of this perverted fundamental decision, which according to Kant constitutes the "radical evil" of the human being, we still, without interruption, always recognize the claims of morality, now as a claim of a moral regeneration or conversion.[48] Kant, however, must here confront the problem of how a human being with an evil fundamental maxim, which determines the choice of all his or her other maxims, can will a conversion to the good at all: "Wenn der Mensch aber im Grunde seiner Maximen verderbt ist, wie ist es möglich, dass er durch eigene Kräfte diese Revolution (der Gesinnung) zu Stande bringe, und von selbst ein guter Mensch werde?" (Rel. B 54). How it can be possible for an evil human being to make himself into a good human being transcends all our concepts: "[…] denn wie kann ein böser Baum gute Früchte bringen ?" (Rel. B 49).

The antinomy sharpens between the claim of a moral regeneration and the impossibility of this regeneration then because of Kant's doctrine of "radical evil". Further, Kant cannot easily refer to any "supernatural contribution" or the cooperation of a "higher power" and the effects of Divine grace because it would seem incompatible with the autonomy of the human being. This autonomy presupposes that moral conversion must be the individual person's own task, and that it cannot be effected by the act of another being:

> Was der Mensch im moralischen Sinne ist, oder werden soll, gut oder böse, dazu muss er sich selbst machen, oder gemacht haben. Beides muss eine Wirkung seiner freien Willkür sein; denn sonst könnte es ihm nicht zugerechnet werden, folglich er weder moralisch gut noch böse sein (Rel. B 48).

The "new creation […] and change of heart" or "rebirth" (Rel. B 54) must be an achievement of the agent himself, and the moral conversion requires a new "highest maxim" (Rel. B 55) through a free act.

---

48 For an account of Kant's doctrine of "radical evil", see Bonaunet 1994 a.

This is incomprehensible, however, as the "radical evil" as "radical" has depraved the "root" (*radix*) of all the maxims of the agent.

Kant attempts in this regard to formulate a conception which implies cooperation between the moral efforts of the agent himself and a Divine grace, but in such a way that the agent's own moral efforts constitute a necessary condition for the hope that God will complete the moral regeneration the agent himself has initiated. But there are reasons to doubt whether Kant can be said to succeed in consistently giving an account of the possibility of a conversion from the human being's propensity or *Hang* to evil, to a good disposition, and of a cooperation between human autonomy and Divine grace.[49] R. Wimmer (1990 p. 159) and L. Mulholland (1991) both have proposed a complementation of Kant's thinking concerning this point, in terms of Erasmus' idea of a first Divine intervention, by which the human being is placed in a position to make a new fundamental choice, which then, however, must be attributed to the agent himself in virtue of his autonomy.[50]

With regard to the problem of the possibility of a moral regeneration, Cohen, at least initially, might assume a better position than Kant, because Cohen rejects the thought of a "radical evil" in the human being: It is, Cohen asserts, rather the good which is radical in the human being (BR 59).The human being is in no way evil "in his essence" or in his "basic drives" ("Grundtriebe") (ibid., cf. also RV 213 f.). "Gott hat seinen heiligen Geist in das Innere des Menschen gesetzt. Der Mensch kann noch so viel sündigen, so kann er doch der Reinheit seiner Seele und seines heiligen Geistes nicht

---

49   For a discussion of the problems of compatibility between autonomy and Divine grace in Kant's philosophy of religion, cf. J. Hare's criticism of what he designates as "Kant's failure" (Hare 1996 p. 60 ff.).
50   See concerning this Bonaunet 1994 b. The affinities between Erasmus' and Kant's thinking on these issues are also treated by E. Galbraith; cf. Galbraith 1996, chapter III, and Galbraith 1997.

verlustig gehen" (BR 105). It is, however, reasonable to ask whether and to which degree Cohen's concept here differs from Kant's.

For, as Cohen himself points out (BR 59), Kant confines the "radical evil" in the human being to "(eine) Verkehrung der Prinzipien", and correspondingly rejects the possibility that a human being could be "diabolical", i.e. such that one did what is evil for the sake of the evil (cf. Rel. B 32).[51] Further, neither is the human being "evil in his essence" according to Kant: To the "essence" of the human being belongs, rather, a "predisposition" ("Anlage") to the good (cf. Rel. B 15 ff.). And because the human "propensity" ("Hang") to evil consists in a "reversal of principles", i.e. of the proper relation between the principles of morality and self-love, the "predisposition" to the good remains intact. It has not been wiped out, but remains as a "seed of goodness, in its full purity" (Rel. B. 50). Without this any moral improvement would be impossible (cf. Rel. B 52). In addition, we should note that "radical evil", according to Kant's interpretation, appears in (three) different degrees, ranging from "frailty" or weakness of will, and "impurity" (insofar as morality in itself does not constitute a sufficient motive to act and self-deception) to deliberate subordination of the moral law under self-love by an act of will. The third degree of evil, Kant asserts, can still be compatible with a will that is generally good, because we in our lives not necessarily need to be involved in situations in which we offend others because we view them as obstacles to our own strivings for a good life.

Yet, in spite of this, Cohen's conception differs from Kant's in certain ways. The individual realizes that all his or her moral efforts are "pieces" ("Stückwerk") only in relation to the sinfulness ("Sündhaftigkeit") one recognizes in the ground of one's being (cf. BR 59).

---

51 R. Wimmer and J. R. Silber both have objections against Kant concerning this issue (cf. Wimmer 1990 p. 120, and Silber 1960 p. cxxv and cxxix).

But the individual's consciousness of a "Sündhaftigkeit" does not imply any evil in his/her essential being (Wesen): "Vielmehr zeugt das Bewusstsein der Sünde gegen die Schlechtigkeit und für die Wacht des Guten" (ibid., cf. also ERW 287). My recognition or consciousness of my "weakness" or "Gebrechlichkeit" testifies in favour of my ethical watchfulness and shows that I am preoccupied with my moral improvement. Further, we ought to note that Cohen thinks differently from Kant concerning the character of this "sinfulness" or "weakness" ("Sündhaftigkeit" or "Gebrechlichkeit") in the human being. As in traditional Jewish understanding Cohen conceives all human sin as *shegagah*, or "unwitting transgression" ("unwissentliches Vergehen") (RV 232, cf. also ERW 346): It is, Cohen asserts, a basic ethical thought that human sin, as the sin in which the human being is and remains a human being is *shegagah*, and that all human sin is "Irrung, [...] Schwanken und Wanken" (RV 234). It is lack of knowledge ("Nichtwissen") that explains the mistakes and failures of the human being: "Der Irrtum, auch die Irrung ist sein Los, daher aber auch die Schegagah die Grenze seines Irrtums" (RV 260). This, Cohen asserts, is the condition for not considering a human being as an animal or a beast ("Unmensch"). Our human self-understanding is at a loss when facing the possibility of the evil in man (ibid.), and with regard to a transgression of this limit and other kinds of morally wrong acts we must, Cohen maintains, search for pathological explanations (cf. RV 234). On this issue Cohen also invokes the ethics of Socrates:

> In dieser Einsicht berührt sich [...] auf das genaueste die monotheistische Religion [...] mit der Ethik in ihrem Ursprung bei Sokrates. Wie Sokrates alle Tugend mit dem Wissen gleichsetzt, alles Unrecht daher als Unwissenheit deutet, so wird [...] die Sünde erklärt als Unwissentlichkeit (RV 232 f.).[52]

---

52 I. Kajon remarks that Cohen with this also reveals his attachment to Maimonides. According to Maimonides there is a necessary connection from

Here Cohen mentions the objection that an understanding like this could seem to conflict with the individual's knowledge of his guilt. It is not completely clear how he lays this objection to rest. On the one hand, he seems to assert that intentional defiance of the moral law is impossible, and that we meet the limits of our self-understanding as accountable agents, as opposed to pathological explanations, by "unwissentliches Vergehen", our acting unknowingly (cf. above). On the other hand, he insists first that the individual's understanding of how he himself is the origin of his guilt is essential for adequate self-knowledge (cf. RV 227 f.; see also above), but also that I, in the first person's perspective, ought not to allow myself an explanation like this, i.e. in terms of acting unknowingly: "[…] diese Erklärung, diese Sicherung des Menschen gegenüber der Verfehlung durfte der Mensch sich selbst nicht geben; er würde sonst seine Selbsterkenntnis schädigen" (RV 234).[53] We should also note how Cohen himself in ERW warned against a levelling of the question of guilt to the "Socratic question of knowledge" and of turning moral guilt into a mistaken thought ("Denkfehler") only (cf. ERW 348 f.).

Cohen also states, as we have seen earlier, that we should operate asymmetrically concerning the imputation of moral guilt to ourselves/to others, as he says it damages our compassion towards oth-

---

knowledge of God as a theoretical activity to love of the human being as an ethical activity, and "a just and good action necessarily arises from the knowledge of ideas of justice and goodness because thought is not an abstract force, but love […] which moves a person […]" (Kajon 2000 p. 214).

53   L. Kaplan attemps to dissolve this apparent inconsistency by Cohen: "It would weaken the individual's moral responsibility […] if he viewed his sin as *shegagah*, as unwitting. Rather, for Cohen, the individual takes full responsibility for his sin, and views it as deliberate. But in the correlation with God, which here takes place in the public […] the sin is deemed by God to be *shegagah* and is forgiven accordingly" (Kaplan 2000 p. 197), (cf. also Poma 1997 p. 222 f.). This dissolution of the inconsistency presupposes a transition to a theological point of view.

ers if we are preoccupied with their guilt (cf. above p. 77). The only sin and weakness that I should seek out is my own: "An mir selbst soll ich die Sünde studieren, und an der Sünde soll ich mich selbst erkennen lernen [...], wie ich selbst in meinem innersten Wesen mit der Sünde behaftet bin" (RV 25). Cohen further points out how: "Der soziologische Standpunkt verfolgt mit Bedacht und Recht den Grund der sittlichen Schäden in den Gegensätzen und Reibungen der soziale Verhältnisse" (RV 210) (see also above p. 76). But the sociological point of view must never be taken as absolute, and ought not to exclude our search for an understanding of the origin of moral evil in the human individual, in the human I (cf. RV 214), and i.e. again in the first person's perspective.[54] And under no circumstance are we allowed to eliminate the question of moral evil by assuming that moral guilt or sin is only an illusion (RV 213).

Against Cohen we could, if he would maintain the idea of ignorance or unknowing actions as a basis for morally wrong acts, object that he then ought to limit the human being's self-knowledge of his or her guilt to apply only to a possible responsibility for one's own ignorance. But this would hardly be compatible with his emphasis on the consciousness of moral guilt as essential to adequate

---

[54] Cf. also BR 118 f.: "Die persönliche Verantwortlichkeit des Individuums, seine Verantwortlichkeit für alle seine Handlungen, seine Pflicht, alle seine Handlungen auf seine sittliche Autonomie hin zu prüfen, zu regeln, zu leiten und zu beleuchten, darf nicht geschmälert werden durch das moderne Bewusstsein von seinem sozialen Schicksal. Seine Verantwortlichkeit kann aber nur dann ernst, innig, fest und stark werden und bleiben, wenn trotz dieser sozialen Einsicht, und gleichsam ihr entgegensetzt das Bewusstsein geweckt wird und wachbleibt: dass jeder Mensch, und wäre er in Ketten geboren, frei ist, sofern er frei sein soll, sofern er sich die Aufgabe stellen soll, frei sein zu wollen". And Cohen emphasizes how the idea of the freedom and responsibility of the human individual is at risk of being suppressed, by the confrontation with the theoretical, "one-sided" doctrine of the sociological determination of the human being.

human self-knowledge. In the last instance, as far as I can see, Kant's doctrine of "radical evil" (Beyond weakness of will, self-deception, and "impurity", a human being consciously and willingly sets aside the moral claims of respect for the Other, if necessary, to fulfil his own interests.) constitutes a more adequate articulation of our self understanding, than a "Socratic" conception of moral mistakes in terms of ignorance. The paragraphs where Cohen does not permit us to understand (from the first person's perspective) our moral shortcomings only in terms of ignorance and our "acting unknowingly", are where, in my opinion, he comes closest to a viable understanding of our *conditio humana* and an adequate "doctrine of the human being" (which is the task of ethics according to Cohen) (cf. e.g. RV 13; see above p. 25 and 38). In some of his formulations Cohen also seems to come very close to Kant's thought of the moral evil as something involving a "fundamental decision" or as Kant says: a fundamental or "highest maxim", which, in its turn, determines our secondary maxims and through those our actions. He emphasizes, for example, how we never ought to understand each sin as an isolated unit, but as connected with an underlying whole in the life of a human being, a "way" according to Cohen's expression, and how: "Jede Einzelsünde ist ein Inbegriff des Menschen, ein Wahrzeichen seines Wesens [...]" (RV 240). But the closer Cohen gets to Kant's conception of the "radical evil", the more accentuated the problem of the possibility of a moral regeneration becomes. Cohen's peculiar perspective of sin having its ground in ignorance, together with his explicit rejection of Kant's thought of the "radical evil" and a corresponding insistence on the idea of the human being as "radically good",[55] implies that he does not, to the same extent as Kant,

---

55 R. Wiehl has (according to P. Schmid, 2000 p. 302) characterized Cohen's denial of the "radical evil" as "eine optimistische Verharmlosung". This consideration does not seem to be entirely unreasonable.

focus on the problems of the possibility of a moral "revolution" of our fundamental dispositions or *Gesinnung*. This does not mean, however, that Cohen entirely neglects to address the problems of removal of and liberation from moral guilt. On the contrary, these problems are discussed thoroughly in BR and RV where Cohen again and again emphasizes how a right self-knowledge must include recognition of moral guilt as something I myself, in virtue of my possession of a rational and free will (Vernunftwille/freier Wille) (cf. RV 195), have incurred.

In what follows, I will account more closely for Cohen's treatment of the problem of moral guilt and his conception of its relevance for the philosophy of religion, and later also in connection with M. Scheler's discussion of similar questions. We must here also have in mind N. Hartmann's problem of whether liberation from guilt is possible without simultaneously revoking the status of the individual as an autonomous person (cf. above p. 78 f.).

Knowledge of guilt, liberation from guilt and "the problem of the individual"

"The problem of the individual" (RV 195) constitutes for Cohen the basis for the idea of transcending ethics and the ethical concept of the human being, moving towards a religious dimension. Within a purely ethical conception, i. e. a conception where the human being – as a rational being – is defined as a moral being and as under the obligation of the claims of morality or "the moral law", we can, according to Cohen, only talk of an "abstract" human individuality. The individual person is here only a "bearer" of "the moral law" to which he or she is subject (cf. RV 192), and a representative or "case" (RV 196) or an "instance" or "example" (cf. BR 52 and RV 17f.) of humanity. Under the aspect of compassion the Other appears for me as a fellow human being, as *Mitmensch* and as *thou*. This implies at the same time a correlation between I and You, which Cohen considers to be a necessary condition for my consciousness of myself as an I (cf. above). This idea of the I, however, as an I in relation to a You, is still, Cohen asserts, incomplete. A complete concept of the human being as an individual and an I requires according to Cohen not only a practical and practical-philosophical approach, as something we are not able to account for within a theoretical-philosophical framework, and, as we could say, merely in terms of a "numerical identity" (cf. Tugendhat 1979 p. 289): It can't be limited only to the concept of the fellow human being and the corresponding "I-you" correlation. A complete "practical I-identity" (cf. Wolf 1984 p. 138 ff.) presupposes also a concept of the individual in relation to her/himself, which is related to one's having to "stand up for oneself" alone (RV 192) and a concept of an "absolute individual" (RV 193 and 196) (cf. above p. 75).

According to Cohen true human individuality presupposes that the human being understands himself first in relation to the state, and next in relation to a universal humanity and as an "individual of humanity" (cf. e. g. RV 208 f. and BR 52 f.). Cohen in his Ethik des reinen Willens even goes so far as to designate the state, and not the human individual as the primary ethical subject (cf. ERW 228 and 268 f.; cf. also Pascher 1993 p. 104 f.).[56] But ethics implies, as we have seen, only an "abstract concept" of the individual, as an "instance of humanity". The *Other* becomes a *"concrete individual"* and "thou" to me through my attitude of compassion. At the same time, another dimension of the *"concrete individual I"* is constituted as I, standing before the suffering Other as You, recognize my inevitable responsibility towards him (cf. RV 19, 153, 164 f. and 170). This is the point of departure for Cohen's approach to a "complete concept"

---

56 Criticising Cohen for an excessive individualistic thinking is therefore mistaken.

of the I as an "absolute individual": Standing before the suffering Other under the claim of compassion, in recognition of my transgressions of the claims of morality and compassion, I acknowledge my individual responsibility. In this recognition I discover myself as related to myself as a "concrete" and "absolute individual", i.e. in my moral responsibility and guilt. The self-knowledge of guilt concerns several aspects of my "practical I-identity" and "concrete individuality". A first consolidation of I-identity is given already in my acceptance of responsibility: *I* did it (cf. above p. 75). Thus guilt cannot be understood as directed to my past, and set up against consciousness of responsibility as something which concerns present and future. Guilt concerns a decisive element in our diachronical moral identity, insofar as the knowledge of guilt constitutes an identity of the moral subject through past, present and future. P. Ricoeur's formulation also captures this dimension in Cohen's thought: "He who *will* bear the blame is the same who *now* takes the act upon himself and he who *has* acted. And the two dimensions, future and past, are linked to the present, […] in the present of confession" (Ricoeur 1992 (1967) p. 230; cf. also Buber 1965 p. 126 and Westphal 1984 p. 75).

Relating this to some of J. Habermas' discussions of the formation of "I-identity" might contribute to clarify what I think is Cohen's position thus far:

(1) Growing into the social surroundings is necessary for constituting ourselves as accountably acting individuals (Habermas 1998 p. 181; 1979 p. 74). The self of the practical self-relation can only constitute itself as an "I will" as a result of socialization within our immediate communities. – This corresponds to Cohen's conception on socialization within the "pluralities" ("Mehrheiten") of family, class and society.

(2) But this "I will" does not yet constitute an individual will "completely able to recognize itself in its own identity" (Habermas 1998 p. 182). A further condition is that the individual sees her/himself

as a member of a "commonwealth of rational beings" and "under the conditions of a universal discourse" (ibid. p. 185 (referring to G. H. Mead)). – We could say this corresponds to Cohen's concept of the "individual of humanity" or "universality" ("Allheit").

(3) This "individual of humanity", however, in terms of I-identity as "I *überhaupt*" (Habermas 1981, II p. 153), "unveils itself in every individual [...] as something universal after all" (Habermas 1998 p. 161, (here referring to Fichte)); "as a person in general the ego is like all other persons" (Habermas 1979 p. 90). It is therefore necessary to understand the identity of the "I" in two complementary aspects, both as universal and as unique (Habermas 1981, II p. 148). This implies that we have to conceive of a determinate individuality beyond, not only mere numeric identity, but also the generic identity of human beings as persons. – This concept still corresponds to the main claims of Cohen's position.

(4) From this point on, however, Habermas and Cohen go in different directions: Habermas appeals to the distinction between the dimensions of morality and ethics (Habermas 1979 p. 94). The "individual of universality" is conceived of in terms of a free, autonomous will in moral self-reflection (Habermas 1998 p. 187 and 191) or self-determination (Habermas 1981, II p. 150 and 155), while "a fully individuated being" must be conceived of in terms of self-realization (ibid. p. 150 and 153) and ethical or existential self-reflection (Habermas 1998 p. 187). According to Habermas an "individuated being", claiming "uniqueness and irreplaceability" can only be conceived of "in light of a considered individual life project" and the "continuity of [...] (his/her) life history" (ibid. p. 186).

> [...] the individual critically appropriates his own life history. [...] I must choose myself as the one who I am and want to be. Life history becomes the principle of individuation, but only if it is transposed by [...] an act of self-choice into an existential form for which the self is responsible (ibid. p. 164 f.; cf. also Habermas 1979 p. 90 f. and 1981, II p. 151 ff.).

Habermas thinks, then, that the individuality of the unique I can only be conceived of in these concepts of the modern tradition from S. Kierkegaard, to whom he here explicitly refers.

Cohen, on the other hand, argues that a genuine and unique *moral* individuality is possible, and indeed necessary. Some interpretations of Cohen read him as exploring a modern "ethical" or "existential" ("Kierkegaardian") conception of individuality (as in M. Zank 1996 p. 284, and (at least implicitly) R. Horwitz 2000 p. 179; see below). I think, however, that these interpretations miss Cohen's main point: The unique, morally responsible individuality Cohen seeks to grasp belongs to a more fundamental level than the (modern) ideal of our different individual ways of self-realization, and constitutes a condition for the possibility of responsible (in Habermas' terminology:) ethical choices of self. As such, Cohen's conception applies also to "pre-modern" cultures, where the way of life still is regulated by collective standards (as e.g. in a traditional Jewish culture, or among e.g. Russian peasants seeking the church's ritual of penance).

Cohen's thinking concerning the formation of the "concrete I" seems, in some regards, to be parallel to S. Kierkegaard's doctrine of the stages of existence. A brief comparison with Kierkegaard could perhaps contribute to bring Cohen's ideas into relief. Cohen and Kierkegaard both focus on a successive formation of an individual self through progressive stages. We find also according to Cohen's thinking three stages, which in certain respects correspond to the aesthetical, the ethical and the religious stages respectively.

Cohen's idea of a transition from an existence as an "empirical individual" in a "sensuous reality", to an existence as an "individual of universality" ("Allheitsindividuum"), i.e. insofar as the individual first understands himself as belonging to the state, and further as a "citizen of universal humanity" ("Staatsbürger der Menschheit"), corresponds to Kierkegaard's thought of a transition from an aesthetical (cf. *aisthesis* = sensation) form of existence to the ethical, as "the universal individual" ("det almene Individ") (EE, SV III, 241). Cohen does not however, as distinct from Kierkegaard (cf. the extensive accounts in *Enten – Eller* and *Stadier paa Livets Vej*), discuss this transition in much detail.

It could further be objected against Cohen that he, because of his limited concentration on the universality dimension of ethics, and corresponding omission, or rather: explicit rejection of any traditional eudaimonistic – ethical concerns, misses out on insights of essential importance with respect to formation of individual identity within the "ethical stage". Kierkegaard's thinking about how the self at the ethical stage comes to be or "gives birth to itself" ("føder sig selv") (EE, SV III, 239); cf. Cohen's "Erzeugung"), and in contrast to the divided multiplicity of desires and possibilities of the aesthetical stage (cf. EE, SV III, 152 and 172) consolidates its particular distinctiveness and concrete identity, contains in this regard important insights. We can not discuss these matters here, but some of the relevant elements are, suggested in the form of keywords: (1) reflecting on and consciously accepting and taking responsibility for oneself as an acting subject, by "relating oneself to oneself" ("forholde sig til sig selv") and "choosing oneself" (as distinct from "creating oneself"); and further (2) by gradually defining oneself, obtaining one's "own, unique history", "concretion" and "continuity", through a realization of one's potentialities, in accordance with one's own decisions of will and in light of a commitment to certain ethical ideals.[57] Point number two, however, is related to a modern ideal of individuality, which, as far as I can see, does not belong to

---

57 This summary of some of Kierkegaard's ideas is indebted to M. Taylor's clear exposition in Taylor 1975, chapter 5. – Kierkegaard's thinking is certainly important as a complementation of some recent works concerning the issues of human identity, as e.g. E. Tugendhat's (1979) and Ch. Taylor's (1985 and 1989). – An interesting treatment of some common features in Kierkegaard and Ch. Taylor is found in P.J. Mehl 1995.

what concerns us here. The "concrete individuality" Cohen seeks to account for, on the basis of compassion and knowledge of guilt, belongs to a different level than the formation of a particular individual identity in terms of a specific set of "strong evaluations" and "hyper goods" with which I identify myself (cf. Ch. Taylor; see on this Bonaunet 1988, and 1993, chapter I and II, 5). The relevant kind of individuality is rather the one which R. Gaita seeks to grasp when he states that: "Parents who mourn a dead child [...] grieve because the one they have lost is irreplacable, but not in the sense in which something is irreplacable because it has characteristics which we will not find elsewhere" (Gaita 1996 p. 18 f.). If this represents an adequate understanding of Cohen's concerns, M. Zank's interpretation of Cohen must be mistaken: Zank connects Cohen to a current in modern thought since Schleiermacher which makes use of religion to secure the reality as something which "medieval thought had not yet even perceived as problematic: 'the individual as I'" (Zank 1996 p. 284). Except that Zank here disregards how the problem of the individuality of the human being is explicitly thematized in mediaeval philosophy (as in Thomas Aquinas (see Bonaunet 1997 p. 128 f.) and in Duns Scotus (see Gilson 1936 (1991) p. 195)),[58] his reading is also problematic with respect to Cohen's (in my opinion justified) claim that he derives the concept of the "concrete individual" from Biblical sources or "the sources of Judaism". Similarly R. Horwitz's account of Cohen's conception of the connection between sin and individuation is mistaken. Horwitz represents Cohen as if he meant: "Sins are human shortcomings. Each person has a different understanding and different desires: they are the *elements which differentiate one person from another*. Actually, sin is what makes one an individual" (Horwitz 2000 p. 179; ital. KB).

---

58 See concerning the theme of the individuality of the human being in mediaeval philosophy in general, Gilson 1936 (1991) Chapter VIII and X.

On the other hand, Kierkegaard does not sufficiently articulate "the ethical" in terms of a universality of humankind. Certainly, he says that:

> Den der betragter Livet ethisk, han seer det Almene, og Den der lever ethisk, han udtrykker i sit Liv det Almene, han gjør sig til det almene Menneske, ikke derved, at han affører sig sin Concretion, thi saa bliver han til slet Intet, men derved, at han iører sig den og gjennemtrenger den med det Almene" (EE, SV III, 236).[59]

But Kierkegaard connects this element of "universality" or *"det almene"* to the fulfilment of "civic duties" ("borgerlige plikter") such as securing for oneself a good position in the society, entering into marriage, etc. (cf. M. Taylor 1975 p. 196 f.), rather than to obligations founded in the "universality of humanity". Universalistic ethical contents in the Kantian sense are, in Kierkegaard's thought, not present until they become articulated within a religious context, and in terms of a "divine command ethics" (as in "Kjerlighedens Gjerninger", cf. on this Quinn 1997 and Rudd 1993).[60]

If we now return to an exposition of Cohen's conception, we find that a further aspect of the self-knowledge of guilt, emphasized in his analysis, concerns the realization that my anti-normative behaviour has separated me from an affirmative relationship with other human beings (cf. Rotenstreich 1996 p. 193), and has led me to "loneliness" ("Vereinsamung") and isolation from the others and the

---

[59] "He who regards life ethically sees the universal, and he who lives ethically expresses the universal in his life, he makes himself the universal man, not by divesting himself of his concretion, for the he becomes nothing, but by clothing himself with it and permeating it with the universal."

[60] A decidedly Kantian reading of the ethical stage by Kierkegaard is however found in A. M. Pieper, 2000 p. 71 ff.

ethical community (cf. BR 53 f.).[61] Parallel to this radical singularity and separatedness from others is also a separation or alienation from myself, – "the experience of being oneself but alienated from oneself" (Ricoeur 1967 p. 8), or being "divided within oneself" (Morris 1976 p. 99 f.).[62] Or in N. Hartmann's formulation: In the knowledge of moral guilt the person is "zweimal vertreten und gleichsam gespalten" (Hartmann: Ethik p. 741). This "disintegration of the unity of the person [...] manifest in moral conflicts" (Tillich ST II p. 61) could reasonably be characterized as due to an "antagonism against oneself" because one has acted against ideals or norms with – and by – which one identifies oneself (cf. Morris 1976 p. 100 f.).[63]

The self-knowledge of guilt, however, ought to be only a stage of transition according to Cohen: The "sinful I" is only a "point of transition"

> für die Erzeugung des neuen, von der reinen Ethik noch nicht erzeugten Ich, so kann es nicht das sündige Ich bleiben. Die Befreiung von der Sünde muss das Ziel werden, durch dessen Erreichung erst das neue Ich zur Erzeugung kommt (RV 218, cf. also 233).

Liberation from recognized sin must at the same time involve a reconciliation of the inner contradictions which hinder the individual from development into a unified I (cf. RV 220 f.) and a reconciliation between man and man (RV 257), and between man and God

---

61   This insight, i. e. concerning how guilt and guilt consciousness implies a separation from the others and an "extreme" (cf. Launay 2000 p. 84) or "radical singularity" is also emphasized in some recent works on the phenomenon of guilt (cf. Gaita 1996 p. 6, 12 and 32, Morris 1976 p. 96 and Westphal 1984 p. 84).
62   Cf. also concerning this Westphal 1994 p. 84; see also Taylor 1985 p. 106.
63   M. Westphal, in connection with this idea of double separation – from community with others and from oneself – refers to Dostoevski's "underground man".

(cf. RV 231 ff.). Liberation from guilt, then, in Cohen's understanding, essentially involves a religious dimension, since the fundamental content of religion lies in the concept of God in correlation to the human being. Cohen's conception of liberation from guilt and reconciliation within the individual human being and in interpersonal relationships, as matters that could only be fully conceived of in connection with the human being's correlation with God (cf. RV 233 ff.), will be the object of our investigations below (p. 114 ff.). For now I will bracket this idea, and also the connected question of the legitimacy of religion.

We should note here, however, how Cohen emphasizes the human being's own responsibility and tasks. Cohen is concerned about the human being's own activity ("Selbsttätigkeit") (RV 232, cf. also BR 63 and 115) and "self-sanctification" (RV (e.g.) 239, 247, 251 and 275) as essential factors and as necessary to preserve human autonomy, which is constitutive for one's ethical dignity (RV 252, cf. also BR 58 and 64):

> [...] wenn es nun [...] gilt die Selbsterkenntnis der Sünde als den Durchgang zu gewinnen für die Befreiung [...] des sittlichen Bewusstseins, so muss bei dem Beschreiten und Durchwandern dieses Durchgangspunktes die Selbständigkeit der Willensarbeit ungehemmt und unbeeinflusst sein von jeder anderen Willenskraft. [...] Jetzt steht [...] der Mensch, als Ich, auf dem Spiele. Und dieses Spiel ist von vornherein verloren, wenn die Selbständigkeit nicht eine absolute wird (RV 236).

Cohen seems to see this way, i.e. from transgression of the claims of morality to recognition of – and liberation from – moral guilt, not only as promoting ethical development and maturation, but in the last instance also as constitutive for the "true" moral individuality of the I (cf. RV 218), and for a complete concept of the human being. It is an important concern for Cohen that the human being through his own sin and knowledge of that sin becomes an *"individual"* (RV 225, cf. also ERW 284). Then through his "self-transformation" (ibid.) and ability to "create for himself a new heart and a new spirit", he becomes an *"I"* or a *"free I"* (cf. RV 218f., 225f. and 233f.), even if he does not always consistently hold on to this terminological distinction and also talks about "the sinful individual" as "the sinful I" (cf. e.g. RV 216 and 218), and that the "I" appears as the human being recognizes him- or herself as the origin of his/her guilt (RV 227f., cf. also 234). This seems reasonable because it is precisely the *I*, as the first person's instance, who is the primary object for attribution of responsibility (cf. above p. 74ff.).

Yet, it is essential to note that Cohen reserves the concept of the I in a special way for the individual who has acknowledged, and is then liberated from his or her guilt. The transformation of the "individual" to an "I" for Cohen is constituted by the inner reconciliation which is essential for the formation of a unified I, in a "Versöhnung des Menschen mit den Widersprüchen, die sein Individuum nicht zur Einheit des Ich kommen lassen" (RV 220, cf. also 225f.). In the recognition of guilt the person is, according to N. Hartmann's expression, "zweimal vertreten und gleichsam gespalten" (Hartmann: Ethik s. 741), (see above concerning the separation of the individual from himself in his guilt). This split is healed through the liberation from guilt and a moral regeneration. A "true individuality of I-ness" (RV 219) is now established, as a (according to P. Tillich's way of expressing this point) "complete centeredness" of the human being (cf. Tillich ST II p. 71). A "true I-ness" or "complete centeredness" as this, however, Cohen emphasizes, is to be conceived as an ideal that can be achieved only by approximation (RV 257), or as "the ideal moment" in a never ending fulfilment, and as such, always a task (RV 238).

An "I-ness" of this kind is a condition, also, for a fully realized relation to the Other as a "concrete individual". And the "reconciled" ethical community is not longer constituted as a mere "universality" ("Allheit") of "abstract" or "only social" individuals, but will be (as Cohen expresses his point in a terminology borrowed in part from

Kant (cf. Rel. B 127 ff.)) "a kingdom of morality" as a "God's kingdom on earth", as a totality of "concrete" individuals as "individual I's", such that in a "world of ends" sociality and individuality will come together (cf. RV 251). Held up against Hartmann's view, that liberation from guilt would abolish the ethical status of the person (cf. above p. 81), we can now, on the basis of Cohen's account of the problem of moral guilt, assert that the process of recognition of guilt and of penance and reconciliation, still founded in the autonomy of the human being, *restores* and *consolidates* the individual in his/her *ethical dignity*, in contrast to his/her "inner dividedness" (cf. Hartmann).[64]

Hartmann asserts that an antinomy exists between ethics and religion (Hartmann: Ethik s. 354), a basic antinomy in which "thesis and antithesis stand in strict contradiction to each other" (ibid. p. 819), i. e., insofar as religion offers a deliverance or redemption, which ethics, because of its basic presuppostions, cannot allow for: "[...] Erlösung [...] ist [...] Abnahme der Sünde, Entlastung des Menschen von ihr, Befreiung, Reinigung, Wiederherstellung des Menschen" (ibid. p. 817). But, Hartmann says, we must realize that: "Das Schuldigsein an der bösen Tat kann niemandem abgenommen werden, weil es unabtrennbar ist vom Schuldigen – man müsste ihm denn das Schuldigsein selbst absprechen und ihm damit die sittliche Zurechnungsfähigkeit bestreiten" (ibid. p. 818, cf. also p. 354). According to Hartmann's comprehension, ethics does not need any resolution of the antinomy because ethics knows of no redemption (cf. ibid. p. 354). To search for such a solution would be a task for the philosophy of religion, a task it will never be able to solve

---

64 Cf. also R. Spaemann who asserts that the possibility of a forgiveness of sin "ist für Personen wesentlich, weil diese Möglichkeit eins ist mit der Möglichkeit, sich als Person durch die Zeit behaupten zu können" (Spaemann 1996 s. 110).

(cf. ibid. and also p. 821). But in light of the preceding account of Cohen, it seems reasonable, *versus* Hartmann, to assert that it is precisely *ethics* that requires a solution of the problem of moral guilt and an understanding of the possibility of reconciliation. If we here discuss an antinomy, it must be the case that it is an antinomy which is generated within ethics itself, insofar as the continued existence of the human being as a person – his or her *Personsein* – is what presupposes and requires redemption or liberation from moral guilt.

A complete synthesis of individual human beings within a "kingdom of ends" and a "completion of the human being in a messianic humanity" (RV 274) seems, according to Cohen, to presuppose "the individual with its sin and its liberation from it" (RV 251), because the "origin of the individual" lies in his or her recognition of his/her own guilt (cf. RV 196). Cohen refers, as mentioned above (p. 77), to Ezekiel as the first to state that sin is the sin of the individual, and as the one who by this "discovers the individual", precisely in his/her sin (cf. RV 214, BR 56 and 61). Or, as M. Launay seeks to summarize Cohen's position: "Dass meine Seele sündigt, begründet erst meine Person, die in der Selbstreflexion ihrer Fehler den Anlass findet, die Prinzipien ihres moralischen Verhaltens zu entwickeln" (Launay 1992 p. 97). Cohen himself raises the objection, however, that his conception here might be "self-contradictory", insofar as it is inconsistent in relation to an ethical-universalistic context and the basic presuppositions of this: "Durch die Sünde soll der Mensch Individuum werden, und zwar als ein seiner selbst bewusstes Ich. Ist das nicht ein Widerspruch?" (RV 234). But Cohen denies that this is the case and rejects the suggestion of a contradiction: "Es ist keiner; denn die Sünde ist die Sünde der Menschlichkeit" (ibid.). He refers again to the thought that the sin which is the issue is a "sin of human weakness" (cf. above p. 86 f.), and further points out how all this concerns our human condition of having to "find our way" through our "human weakness". Thus, "the stage of sin" is "ein unentsetzbares Glied in der Begriffskette des sittlichen Menschen" (BR 65).

Cohen's concerns here, however, are probably are more comprehensive: His account of the individual and its suffering (cf. below p. 110 ff.) has explicitly the function of a theodicy (cf. concerning this, Schulte 1997). But as far as I can see, it is reasonable to assert that Cohen sets forth his theodicy-thinking already here, and in relation to the problem of God creating a being who not only has the possibility of ethical errors, but who actually makes morally wrong choices and performs wrong actions. Cohen's answer amounts to pointing out how the individual only can be generated by a "negative condition" (cf. Launay 2000 p. 83), and how, as P. Schmid formulates Cohen's conception: "Die Sünde selbst bringt das Individuum erst in seiner vollen Bestimmung zur Entdeckung" (Schmid 2000 p. 293). If this interpretation is correct, it is not difficult to see serious problems in Cohen's argument unless one, with Cohen, conceives of sin and moral guilt exclusively in terms of *shegagah* and human weakness. But an understanding like this is hardly viable. We can ask along with P. Natorp in his notes of his reading of BR: Are the atrocities of war an indispensible and legitimate part of the development towards "true" individuality? (Cf. Natorp's remark: "Krieg – das durchgreifende Mittel, damit die Welt des Friedens aufblühen kann" (Natorp 1986 (1915) p. 116)). A "Cohenian" theodicy, in this regard, does not make any contribution to the solution of this issue beyond attempts to give an answer to the problem of evil in terms of the indispensability of creating the human being as a being of freedom, while it implies some considerable problems of its own.

*The phenomenology of the knowledge of –
and redemption from guilt*[65] *(Cohen and Scheler)*

It is interesting to note both the basic agreements and divergences between Cohen's account of the different stages of the process from recognition of guilt to liberation from guilt, which he elaborates through his reading of the "sources of Judaism", and M. Scheler's corresponding phenomenological description (cf. Scheler VEM, 1. Part: "Von Reue und Wiedergeburt").

For Cohen, remorse ("Reue") is the "preliminary stage" and a "negative condition" ("Vorbedingung") for a process of "penance" towards redemption and liberation from guilt. Remorse is, according to Cohen's analysis, an "expression of feeling" and an "affect" which accompanies my dissociation from my "old way of life". By itself, this feeling can only lead to despair, and, as such, it is not "creative". "Creativity" is not present until my recognition and confession of my guilt: "Helles Bewusstsein in Erkenntnis und Handlung, darauf kommt es an, und darin wird der Grund gelegt für den neuen Lebensbau" (RV 237). In another context we find, however, that Cohen avoids separating "remorse" and "confession": "Bekenntnis und Reue gehen [...] ineinander über. So ist die Reue [...] in voller Wirksamkeit, wenn das Bekenntnis sich losringt" (RV 254). This idea, which tends to merge remorse and confession, is in accordance with Scheler's: "Readiness" to remorse is necessary for a truthful self-knowledge, and the person who repents of his act will also confess it (VEM 21). In this way, a "readiness to confession" necessarily grows out of remorse (cf. ibid. 39).[66]

---

65   Cf. Ricoeur's concept of "a phenomenology of confession" as "a description of meanings and [...] intentions, present in a certain activity of language: the language of confession" (Ricoeur 1992 (1967) p. 224).

66   Cf. also, in this respect, Ricoeur who also emphasizes how the confession of sin is "embedded in the matrix of emotion, fear, [...] anguish", but at the

Scheler's account of the phenomenon of guilt contains moments which are in fundamental agreement with the ideas of Cohen and Hartmann, as these have been explicated above: Moral guilt is, in Scheler's opinion, a "quality" which is attached to the person who violates his or her moral obligations:

> Schuld ist jene Qualität "böse", die der Person selbst, dem Aktzentrum, durch ihre bösen Akte [...] zugewachsen ist. Eine Qualität also, nicht aber ein "Gefühl" ist die Schuld. [...] "Schuldgefühl" [...] (ist eine) innere Sinnbeziehung auf diese Qualität. [...] Ob man sich also auch schuldig fühle oder nicht – die Schuld haftet (VEM 39).

It is this "objective quality of guilt" towards which remorse is directed, and which constitutes its "intentional object", and not the *feeling* of guilt, even if remorse is directed towards guilt "through" the feeling of guilt (VEM 40). Scheler further distinguishes between what he designates as "Tatreue", which concerns the particular act, and "Seinsreue", which concerns the ethical quality of the agent. According to Scheler's idea, every "Tatreue" must, in the last instance, lead to "Seinsreue" (cf. VEM 24 f. and 29). Or rather: Every "Tatreue", in the last instance, *is* "Reue über das Verschuldetsein der Person durch die Tat" (VEM 41). Cohen also emphasizes how sin ought not to be understood in terms of isolated singular acts, but must be connected with a more comprehensive context, forming a more

---

same time – in line with Cohen's emphasis of "helles Bewusstsein in Erkenntnis und Handlung" – points out how "through confession man remains speech, even in the experience of his own absurdity, suffering and anguish" (Ricoeur 1967 p. 7). Cf. further R. Gaita who does not conceive of remorse as an emotional effect of the knowledge of guilt, but rather as the primary form of this knowledge: "Remorse is not recognition plus suffering: it is the indivisible suffering-recognition of the meaning of what one did" (Gaita 1996 p. 6, referring to Wittgenstein).

unitary whole – a "way" – in Cohen's mode of expression (cf. above p. 14).[67]

Scheler further points out, still in accordance with the ideas of Cohen (and Hartmann), how my insight into my guilt accentuates my self-knowledge as a being of freedom: "Wir "konnten" auch anders sein, [...] wollen und handeln. (Der Reueakt) [...] zeigt uns [...] dieses "können", diese zentralste Willensmacht" (VEM 26). And: "Erst im Reueakt geht uns [...] die volle evidente Erkenntnis

---

67 Cf. also BR 62 where Cohen says that the question of moral guilt is not directed towards any singular "station" within the life of a human being, "sondern gleichsam auf sein ganzes Menschenleben". B. Williams seems to assert that guilt does not involve any "conceptions of what one is and how one is related to others", while this is something which belongs to shame, as different from guilt (cf. Williams 1994 p. 92 f.). Cf. also G. Taylor 1985 p. 89: "Feelings of guilt [...] concern themselves with the wrong done, not with the kind of person one thinks one is", (cf. also ibid. p. 92). Correspondingly, she asserts that remorse is concentrated on the action which has been performed, rather than on the agent her- or himself. Further, she states that "Remorse is not an emotion of self-assessment" (ibid. p. 99 f.). The concept of "Seinsreue" would, from the perspective of the conceptions of Williams and Taylor seem to be a mistaken construction. I can not find, however, either in Williams or Taylor, any observations that should require us to reject the conceptions of Scheler (and Cohen) in this respect. Within recent Anglo-American analyses of the phenomenology of guilt, H. Morris has a concept which is more similar to Scheler's and Cohen's, when he refers to a transition from focussing on one's singular actions to "taking more seriously who [...] (one) presently is and who [...] (one) will be", and therefore "a concern with (a) fundamental change" (Morris 1976 p. 109). As opposed to Williams' characterization of the distinction between guilt and shame, I think Habermas succeeds much better in spelling out the basic differences, insofar as he sees shame as connected to nonconformity to external rules, while guilt is generated by a transgression of the internalized norms of conscience (see Habermas 1979 p. 76 and 81).

jenes Gekonnthabens eines Bessern auf" (VEM 27).[68] But while Cohen conceives of remorse as a feeling which is not "creative" unless it leads further to acts of knowledge and confession (cf. above), Scheler asserts that *knowledge*, in this respect, "creates nothing": "sie ist Erkenntnis, [...] sie zeigt nur an [...]" (ibid.). For Scheler, remorse in itself, beyond its negative "reprehensive" function, already has a positive function as "liberating" and "edifying" (cf. VEM 7 and 43), as "eine Form der Selbstheilung der Seele, ja der einzige Weg zur Wiedergewinnung ihrer verlorenen Kräfte" (VEM 12) and to a new "freedom to the good" (VEM 29). We can also understand how Scheler could see remorse and knowledge of guilt as capabilities or powers which represent the "radical good" (Cohen) in the human being, when he said that we through these at the same time are able to see "eine ganz höhere, idealische Existenz als eine für uns mögliche" (VEM 27) and when he talks about "die Mitgegebenheit eines idealisches Wertbildes [...] unserer Person (im Reueakt)" (VEM 36), or about "[...] (ein) positives Leitbild des Selbstseins und Selbstwerdens" (VEM 37).[69]

Scheler's phenomenological description is, however, less detailed and differentiated than the account by Cohen. In Scheler's analysis, it is remorse ("Reue") that carries the entire process to liberation from guilt: Remorse brings about an annulment of guilt and cancels its continued effects or "Fortwirksamkeit" (VEM 38), "vernichtet wahrhaft jene psychische Qualität welche "Schuld" heisst. [...] Sie

---

68 Cf. again Ricoeur 1992 (1967) p. 230 f.: "[...] the experience of remorse [...] is the experience of the relation between freedom and obligation", by which "I designate myself as he who not only performed the act but who could have done otherwise".

69 Scheler rejects with intensity what he characterizes as "Kant's terrible old-protestantic doctrine" of "radical evil" (cf. VEM 434).

macht [...] damit neue, schuldfreie Anfänge des Lebens möglich" (VEM 41, cf. also 17 f. and 30). Corresponding to this, Scheler describes remorse as a "mighty power of self-regeneration" of "the soul" or "the moral world" (VEM 41, cf. also 43 f.). The object of remorse is, as mentioned above, the guilt which is imputed to me. But its purpose or aim is "Vorsatzfassung" (VEM 36), "Gesinnungsänderung und Gesinnungswandel, [...] das 'neue Herz'. [...] All dies quillt aus der Reue hervor" (VEM 42). In one context, Scheler mentions what he refers to as different "beliefs" and "dogmatic concepts" which concern the various steps or stages within this process, such as (beyond "remorse") "confession", "penance", "justification", "reconciliation" and "sanctification" (VEM 50), but he avoids any detailed discussion of these issues, because, he claims, it is *remorse* that constitutes the foundation and the "simple root" of these beliefs.

Cohen, on the contrary, gives an account of these within the framework of "a phenomenology of the various stages of conversion" (Poma 1997 p. 221). He divides the entire process of liberation from guilt, which he grasps under the designations of "penance" ("Busse") or "self-sanctification" in four stages, and characterizes these in traditional religious terms as (1) "remorse", (2) scrutinizing one's "entire way of life" ("Lebensweg"), (3) "conversion" ("Umkehr") and (4) creating of a "new way of life" (cf. RV 239 f.). As we have seen above, remorse, according to Cohen, constitutes a preliminary emotional stage for "self-examination" or self-knowledge and confession of guilt. But this, in turn, only constitutes a stage of transition: "Denn bei der Erkenntnis der Sünde darf es nicht sein Bewenden haben. Sie muss nur der Anstoss werden, dass der Mensch von der Last der Sünde frei werde" (RV 222). There is a difference, Cohen states, between "examining one's way" and "turning away" from it: "Das Durchprüfen ist Vorbedingung, unerlässliche, aber nicht mehr. Das Abwälzen aller Sünden ist die neue Kraft, in der das Ich ins Leben tritt [...]. das neue Ich" (RV 237; cf. also 218 f., 233, 236 and 239). The third and the fourth stages are, then, decisive as moments of a moral regeneration.[70]

Confession of guilt as a "speech act"

According to Cohen, it is essential that the recognition of guilt, as a performative act and different from an "observation" (cf. Ricoeur 1992 (1967) p. 230) or a "theoretical interpretation" (cf. Schaeffler 1989 p. 55), as also prayer, has the character of, in Cohen's terminology, a "speech act" ("Sprachhandlung") (RV 463; cf. also ERW 185 and 187), by which I constitute myself as a "responsible will" (Ricoeur 1992 (1967) p. 237) or as a "practical subject" (cf. Schaeffler 1999 p. 94), within a concrete dialogue community, as a community which at the same time becomes consolidated by this speech act. Confession is not then a matter which could be restricted to and be carried through "in der Stille und im Geheimnis des Menschenherzens" (RV 228). "Die Busse [...] soll eine reale, eine realisierende Handlung des Willens sein, welche den Menschen zum Ich-Individuum emporhebt" (RV 236). We can understand this as

---

70 A philosophical analysis as (e.g.) Cohen's of course implies a considerable degree of abstraction and schematizing in relation to the complexity of our concrete human moral lives. And it will hardly be the case that we in our actual experience go through a continuous linear progressive development in accordance with the four stages of Cohen's enumeration. F. Dostoevski's extensive descriptions in "Crime and Punishment" of Raskolnikov's "process of regeneration", with its ruptures and relapses, towards a point where he (and we) can sense a hope of reconciliation, constitute an illustration which much better captures the complexity of our lived experience. But this literary depiction in no way makes redundant the more abstract philosophical approaches of Cohen, Scheler and others. Rather, the two modes of approaching these problems mutually complement each other.

a requirement of a confession to the one I have insulted or offended, and so as part of restoring the relationship with the Other. But, finally, it is, according to Cohen, the confession of sin within a liturgical – religious community which constitutes the relevant speech act. This community must be a historical – concrete language community, which, however, at the same time always has to be directed towards a universal (messianic) dialogue community (cf. Schaeffler 1981 p. 65 and 1989 p. 43; cf. also Ollig 1994 p. 117 ff.). This conception is basically in agreement with Kant's idea of the importance of the task and legitimacy of any church, i.e. insofar as it works as a concrete community towards the realization of a universal ethical community as a regulative idea (cf. Kant's Rel., 3. Stück). By this we also realize how Cohen's philosophy defends the individual against being "dissolved" in a "supra-individual reason", while it at the same time avoids a "privatistic" idea: the individual "[…] remains referred to the community, its history and its service to a future humanity" (Schaeffler 1999 p. 94).

Cohen on penance and suffering. (A (failed) theodicy)

According to Cohen, a readiness to see suffering as a purifying punishment must be included in the human being's "work of penance" (cf. e.g. BR 68 f.). The idea is not that there is any causal connection between moral guilt and suffering as a punishment. The idea, therefore, has no application beyond a first person's perspective (cf. BR 72): It is only I myself who, from the knowledge of my moral guilt, can comprehend my suffering as if it were a deserved punishment (BR 69; cf. Schulte 1997 p. 217). The "self-sanctification" of the human being achieves its summit, Cohen asserts, in the insight of the necessity of suffering, "in dieser freiwilligen, opferfreudigen Hingebung an das Leiden der Strafe" (RV 265, cf. also RV 228, and BR 68 f.). The purifying suffering is already partly present in the recognition and confession of guilt "mit aller Pein und Not in aller Zerknirschung und an Verzweiflung grenzenden Selbstverurteilung" (RV 228, cf. also ERW 357).[71] But Cohen's view does not seem to be that the suffering should be limited to the pain which belongs to and, in part, constitutes remorse and guilt feeling, "das der Reue als solcher anhaftende Leiden" (Scheler VEM 22, cf. also 38) and which is associated with the separation and inner alienation which belong to the knowledge of guilt (cf. above p. 98), or is connected with the confession of guilt (cf. Morris 1976 p. 99 ff.): "Das Leiden im Menschen ist eine Tatsache. [...] Sie wird verständlich, wenn das Leid als *Strafe* erkannt wird" (BR 69; ital. KB).

Cohen's reflections, in this regard, are at the same time a part of a theodicy:

> [...] so klärt sich auch die Korrelation von Gott und Mensch als Theodizee auf. Die Leiden [...] widerstreiten nicht dem gnädigen Gotte [...]. Der Mensch nimmt das Leiden als Strafe auf sich. Dadurch verblasst die Strafe; als Leiden verklärt sie Gott wie Mensch [...]. Das Leiden, es bildet kein Fragezeichen mehr gegen das Wesen Gottes, noch auch gegen das der Menschen. [...] Das Leid gehört als Strafe zum ethischen Begriffe des Menschen (BR 69 f.).[72]

C. Schulte remarks counter Cohen's reasoning in this regard: "Ich halte dieses Theorem "ich bin schuldig, also kann ich ruhig leiden", oder schlimmer noch in der Rückschluss-Version "ich leide, also muss ich wohl auch schuldig sein" für masochistisch" (Schulte 1997 p. 219). On the other hand, it might seem as if having a "need" for

---

71 Cf. N. Hartmann's statement on how carrying guilt can involve "tiefe Unlust, Schmerz, seelische Not, ja direkt Strafe [...], – und wohl öfter, als man glaubt, eine furchtbare Strafe" (Ethik p. 819).

72 O. Leaman's assertion that: "It seems clear that for Cohen there is no theodicy which will explain the suffering of individuals" (cf. Leaman 1995 p.161) is obviously incorrect.

a just punishment for guilt, when one is "struck" by the suffering of the Other whom one has offended,[73] constitutes a fundamental feature of the human existence, and that recognition of one's guilt implies "an affirmative attitude toward the verdict which renders liable to punishment" (Westphal 1984 p. 77). This thought that "the sentiment of guilt [...] is mingled with the anticipation of [...] punishment", also appears in different contexts in P. Ricoeur (cf. Ricoeur 1992 (1967) p. 227, and 1967 p. 41 f.). M. Westphal explicitly objects that "it would be begging important questions simply to label guilt masochistic on account of this" (Westphal 1984 p. 256 n 18).

---

73 Cf. also M. Launay (2000 p. 84 f.), who with regard to this idea refers to Dostoevski's *The Possessed*. This is however a central motive also in other works of Dostoevski. G. Kjetsaa summarizes in an excellent way how this is treated in *The Brothers Karamazov*, where the value of suffering is especially articulated in Sosima's world view. Dostoevski's main concern, in this respect, is the suffering a human being freely and consciously accepts or takes upon himself. "The ability to suffer becomes [...] a moral quality which drives the human being forwards to self understanding and gives him the possibility of purification and transformation." "If suffering for Dostoevski also is a result of sin, it is [...] a *positive* result." "Suffering becomes a necessary psychological condition to get forgiveness for sin", and by freely accepting and subjecting oneself to suffering one "achieves a right to forgive oneself". Further, Kjetsaa asserts, referring to the epitaph of the book (Joh. 12.24), Dostoevski in *The Brothers Karamazov* shows "how evil becomes a basis for the growth of the good, and how decay is a necessary presuppostion for liberation of the energies of life", insofar as the murder of Fjodor Karamazov simultaneously represents "the clearest expression of the decay of life", and also becomes "a condition for the possibility of new life". In the figure of Dimitri Karamazov we can see especially how "his fall and acceptance of suffering becomes a necessary condition for his rebirth" (see Kjetsaa 1985 p. 354 ff. (translations here are mine)). Although there certainly are differences between Dostoevski's understanding and Cohen's, we can sense here, I think, a deep spiritual affinity between these two thinkers. On the "ethics of suffering" in Dostoevski's works, see also Scanlan 2002 p. 110 ff.

A conception like Cohen's can, in some respects, be seen as connected to Kant's idea of being "worthy to happiness" (cf. Kant: KPV A 198 and 234) (cf. Westphal 1984 p. 76f.), and something could be said for it to the extent that Kant's idea has some credibility; Cohen, however, would deny the legitimacy of any connection to the eudaimonistic motive in Kant's thought. Further, one could try to defend Cohen's idea of accepting suffering as a punishment, insofar as one could understand the disposition to accept suffering as something one deserves as evidence of one's genuine remorse and willingness to restoration (cf. Morris 1976 p. 106f.). But this does not mean that Cohen's reasoning is viable as a theodicy. As Kant observed, the problem is that there does not seem to exist any proportionality between moral worthiness or guilt and happiness/suffering. This observation is, as is well known, a foundation of Kant's postulate of the existence of God, as a condtion for the possibility of a realization of the highest good (concerning this, see Bonaunet 1993 p. 471ff.). Correspondingly, neither does Cohen's theodicy answer the question of why suffering – and suffering of just this scope – strikes this individual (me) here and now. And Cohen here seems to miss out on the meaning of Job's problem and the question of the suffering of the innocent (cf. Schulte 1997 p. 219). Finally, doubts of the kind that Natorp raises against Cohen, which we have referred to above (p. 103), will be relevant also, particularily, here. As P. Tillich states:

> There are forms of suffering which destroy the possibility of the subject's acting as subject, as in cases of psychotic destruction, dehumanizing external conditions, or a radical reduction in bodily resistance. Existence is full of instances in which no meaning can be found in suffering on the part of the suffering subject (Tillich ST II p. 71).

The problem of guilt, the irreducibility of the individual and the legitimacy of religion

Cohen's account of the problems of the individual and his/her "redemption" (RV 219) or "reconciliation" (RV 220) and liberation from guilt belongs within the framework of a project which aims in the last instance at a legitimation or a transcendental philosophical justification of religion (cf. above, I, 2). Religion is "given" as a fact (a "fact of culture"). What is at stake is proving its "Rechtsgrund", the foundation for its right to be and to continue to be a component of our human culture (cf. Natorp 1986 (1915) p. 445). According to Cohen's Kantian approach, this foundation must primarily be searched for in ethics, and more precisely in connection with a demarcation of the limits of ethics: "An [...] (der) Grenze der philosophischen Ethik, wo Sünde, Schuld und Leid auftreten, erfolgt der Überschritt zur Religion" (Löwith 1968 p. 365). But what exactly are the limitations of ethics, which Cohen claims require a transition to religion?

According to Cohen's idea, ethics has inherited its essential contents from monotheistic religion (for Cohen: primarily Judaism). But philosophical ethics has the capacity to make these contents its own and justify its fundamental tenets. Cohen then poses the question if, however, there are insights that are essential for an adequate self-understanding of our human ethical existence, having their origin in religion that ethics itself is not able to integrate within its own boundaries, even if they are insights of essential importance for problems having their origin within ethics (BR 43), and which ethics therefore cannot reject.

To clarify Cohen's idea of a "transcendental deduction" of religion, it is important to emphasize that his purpose is not, through philosophy, to generate a "religion of reason" (cf. above p. 11). Religion exists already, with its "sources", meaning its practices and complexes of experiences and ideas. The question, then, is how much of these contents can ethics appropriate and account for? Further:

if there are elements ethics itself can not treat, but at the same time cannot dismiss, such elements, then, "zwar im bleibenden Zusammenhang mit der Ethik, aber über ihre Probleme hinaus" (RV 193) will be contents of a "religion of reason".

We have previously mentioned how Cohen considers what he calls "the messianic God", the one God in relation to one universal humanity, as a "God of ethics" (p. 36; cf. also BR 77 and 116). What Cohen designates as "the God of religion" he conceives of in terms of a relation or "correlation" between God and the individual: between God as the one and "unique" ("einzige") being and the "individual human being" in her or his own "uniqueness" ("Einzigkeit"). And it is, Cohen argues, in the final instance only within the context of religious practice and a "correlation" with God as "unique" ("einzig") that we are able to transform the ethical concept of a human being as an "abstract individual", and as only a "representative" of universal humanity into a "living and individual human creature", and fully understand the existence of an "absolute individual" (RV 193). "Die Eigenart der Religion, trotz ihres unerschütterlich bleibenden Zusammenhanges mit der Ethik, wird erst dadurch in Vollzug treten, dass die Korrelation von Gott und Mensch die engere Bedeutung zum Menschen, als Individuum und als Ich, annimt" (ibid.). The "peculiarity" of religion in relation to ethics consists in the presence of the human being as an individual and as an "I", in connection with a new concept of God, distinct from the idea of "the God of ethics" (RV 216), and in terms of a "correlation" "unique man"/"unique God" ("einziger Mensch"/"einziger Gott") (cf. BR 61). "[…] die Einzigkeit […] fällt ganz aus dem Rahmen der Ethik heraus. Hier muss der Überschritt zur Religion eintreten" (ibid.).

We have discussed Cohen's conception of how the complementation of the ethical claim of universal respect by compassion ("Mitleid") requires a transition from ethics to religion. In what follows we will discuss his conception of the relevance of the correlation God/human being and the importance of religion with its "peculiarity" in relation to ethics, with regard to how this relates to the problem of knowledge of and liberation from moral guilt. For, as Cohen asserts: "In der Lösung dieser Frage [...] vollzieht sich die Eigenart der Religion bestimmt [...] und deutlich [...]" (RV 193).

The problem of moral guilt can reasonably be seen as originating from the basis of ethical categories (see above p. 73 ff.). If Cohen could show that this problem only can be fully understood and coped with in categories of religion, he would have redeemed his claim that here we find ourselves at the limits of ethics, where ethics is in touch with religion and requires a transition to religion itself (RV 195), while at the same time, religion remains closely related to ethics, or remains "unshakeably" connected to ethics (cf. RV 183 f., 196 and 216; cf. also (e.g.) BR 66 and 116 f.). The decisive question then is whether, and in which sense, this could be said to be the case. We must also expect that his explorations will give an account of the existence of the human being as a concrete, unified individual or I, in correlation with God.

The point of departure for Cohen's argument is my self-knowledge of guilt and the consequent moral despair. Ethics with its call to moral universality, he asserts, has no means to help us cope with this (BR 62). "Das Individuum fühlt sich von seiner Sünde beschwert. Da soll ihm nun die Ethik helfen mit ihrem Aufruf zur Allheit" (BR 55).

> Die Ethik kann [...] von dieser Verzweiflung nicht befreien. [...] Was fängt sie [...] mit dem armen Menschen an, der sich seiner Schuld nicht entledigen darf, sofern für sein [...] Bewusstsein der Vernunftwille, der freie Wille bestehen bleiben muss? (RV 194 f.; cf. also 218).

We are, Cohen continues, not able to conceive how a human being, neither in relation to himself, nor in intersubjective correlations with other human beings can meet this problem and be redeemed from (the consciousness of) his guilt. The individual human being, as belonging to a "kingdom of moral beings" has no right to liberate himself from his moral guilt (cf. RV 195 f.). Neither do we see any possibility of how an ethical community could effect a redemption from guilt. In other words, according to Cohen, there exists no human "court" which could "manage" a liberation from moral guilt. Further, Cohen's idea seems to be that merely human conditions are too insecure to carry a trust in a fulfilment of reconciliation with others, because the person in question would be totally subject to their arbitrary will (cf. Launay 2000 p. 84 and 86). – "[…] und da stellt die Korrelation von Mensch und Gott die einzige Möglichkeit zum Beistand dar" (RV 195).

It might be interesting here (again; cf. also above p. 94 ff.) to notice some similarities between Cohen and Kierkegaard. In spite of their differences in conceptions of "the ethical", Cohen and Kierkegaard seem to meet each other in the belief that a merely ethical form of life is insufficient, because ethics does not possess the resources to handle the shortcomings of the agent in relation to the ideality claims of ethics. And although they are taken out of their context here, some of Kierkegaard's statements could also well express essential features of Cohen's conception:

> Ethiken viser Idealiteten som Opgave, og forudsætter at Mennesket er i Besiddelse af Betingelserne. Herved udvikler Ethiken en Modsigelse, i det den netop gjør Vanskeligheden og Umueligheden tydelig (BA, SV V, 115).
>
> […] derfor er det da ogsaae umuligt, at Nogen kan skrive en Ethik uden at have ganske andre Kategorier i Baghaanden. Synden tilhører da kun forsaavidt Ethiken, som det er paa dette Begreb den strander ved Angerens Hjælp. Skal Ethiken påtage Synden, da er dens Idealitet forbi. […] Der er fremkommen en Kategorie, der ligger aldeles udenfor dens Omfang (ibid., 116 f.).[74]

[74] "Ethics points to ideality as a task and assumes that man is in possession of the requisite for performing it. Thereby ethics develops a contradiction, precisely for the fact that it makes the difficulty and the impossibility clear". – "[…] (therefore) no one can write an ethics without having entirely different categories up his sleeve. Sin belongs to ethics only in so far as upon this concept it founders by the aid of repentance. If ethics must include sin, its ideality is lost […] There has come to the fore a category which lies entirely outside its province."

And further: "Saasnart Synden kommer frem, da gaaer Ethiken til Grunde, netop paa Angeren; thi Angeren er det høieste ethiske Udtryk, men netop som saadan den dypeste ethiske Selvmodsigelse" (FB, SV V, 89).[75] For Kierkegaard also, the "category of sin" ("Syndens Kategori"), is the category of the individual or of "singularity" ("Enkelthedens Kategori") (SD, SV XV, 168 f.). We find, however, a decisive difference between their views in that Cohen, unlike Kierkegaard, unambiguously thematizes the religious as a realm that could never and under no conditions imply a "teleological suspension of the ethical" (cf. FB, SV V, 51 ff.), but rather as something which constitutes a "continuation" of ethics (cf. BR 58), and such that "nur im innigsten Anschluss an die Autonomie und nur unter ihrer strengsten Aufrechthaltung kann der religiöse Gott der Gott der ethischen Menschen werden" (BR 116).[76]

As we have already suggested above (p. 99), it is essential for Cohen that the question of liberation from guilt is not treated in a way that excludes the autonomy of the human being (RV 235 f., 262 f. and 276). He refers to the entire process of "penance" as a "self-sanctification" of the human being (e.g. RV 239) and "self-

---

[75] "As soon as sin makes it appearance, ethics comes to grief precisely upon repentance; for repentance is the highest ethical expression, but precisely as such it is the deepest ethical self-contradiction."

[76] Correspondingly, it must be a necessary criterion for every true religion that it is conceived and acted on in accordance with basic principles of ethics and of autonomy (cf. Kant's remarks on the narrative of Abraham's willingness to sacrifice Isaac in Rel. (B 290)). – Cf. in this connection also Kant's remark in "Das Ende aller Dinge": "Sollte es mit dem Christentum einmal dahin kommen, dass es aufhörte liebenswürdig zu sein (welches sich wohl zutragen könnte, wenn es statt seines sanften Geist, mit gebieterischer Auktorität bewaffnet würde), so müsste […] eine Abneigung und Widersetzlichkeit gegen dasselbe die herrschende Denkart der Menschen werden" (Kant: Ende (Werke, Hg.: Weischedel, Bd. XI, 190)).

purification" (e.g. RV 232) which demands a mobilizing of all the strength of the individual (RV 246 f.) and says that the reconciliation toward which the individual must strive must be man's own, independent work (cf. RV 220). The human being is able to choose a new "way of life" ("Lebensweg") and has the capability to create for himself "a new heart and a new spirit" (RV 226) by his own "self-activity" ("Selbsttätigkeit") (RV 232). Cohen also says that the liberation from guilt, in a sense, must be a "self-liberation" (RV 233).

This position seems to exclude any Divine cooperation (cf. RV 236), and it becomes hard to understand the sense in which the process of penance, as Cohen asserts, must be something that takes place "before God" who forgives sin, even if not as "through God" or "with God" (cf. ibid.). At the same time, it might seem as if Cohen's emphasis on human autonomy correspondingly undermines his claim of a transition from ethics to religion altogether. On the other hand, Cohen also has dismissed the possibility of a merely anthropological approach to the problem of liberation from moral guilt. Thus his position apparently ends up in an *aporia*.

Cohen's attempted solution consists in arguing that it is necessary to postulate God as the Being who ensures that man's moral strivings will reach their goal. Nothing in humanity by itself, or within the limits of human existence alone, can provide any foundation for a reasonable hope of a human being's real redemption from guilt. "Wie konnte dies aber menschlich gedacht werden?" (RV 246). "Ihm kann daher nur Gott helfen. Die Güte Gottes bleibt seine einzige Zuflucht. Sie wird daher seine Zuversicht. So entsteht das Vertrauen zu Gott" (RV 247, cf. also BR 104 f.). This does not, however, make man's own labour superfluous: God must, according to Cohen, be thought of as the One who "effects" the redemption or reconciliation (cf. RV 232, 235 and 242 f.). Or rather: What God performs is the "success" ("Erfolg") of redemption, as distinct from the "bringing about" of redemption ("die Herbeiführung der Erlösung") as the independent action of the human being (RV 237). And this ought not to restrain man's own serious autonomous striving for penance and reconciliation (cf. RV 237, 240 f. and 249 f.; BR 63 f.). In this connection, Cohen talks about God as a "support" ("Beistand"), and not as a "collaborator" ("Mitarbeiter") or "collaborating helper" ("mitwirkender Helfer") (RV 240 f.). In this way perhaps Cohen wishes to distance himself from the traditional Christian understanding of the relation between the human being as an autonomous agent and the grace of God in terms of *synergeia* (cf. also RV 400), which, according to Cohen, represents the best that Christianity can come up with (ERW 273), since Cohen found redemption "from without" (ERW 287) a highly offensive idea.[77] But it is not obvious how Cohen, distinguishing between "Herbeiführung der Erlösung" (possibly without "Erfolg") and "Erfolg" (as complementing "Herbeiführung"), and characterizing God as "Beistand" rather than as "Mitarbeiter", succeeds in formulating a different position.

In any case, that God's forgiveness presupposes man's "self-sanctification" is of essential concern for Cohen, as it was for Kant (cf. Rel. B 171 ff., and also 49 f. and 62 ff.), to ensure that the idea of God's forgiveness should not imply any depreciation of the dignity of the human being grounded in its autonomy. At the same time, for Cohen, the human being's reconciliation with God presupposes reconciliation between the involved human beings: "[…] ohne den Frieden mit meinem Mitmenschen kann ich auf keine Versöhnung mit Gott hoffen und auf keinen Frieden in meinem Innern" (Löwith 1968 p. 375 f.). But we cannot be indifferent to the

---

[77] Concerning the relation between Kant's conception of autonomy and the possibility of a Divine contribution or cooperation, and traditional Christian conceptions of freedom (*autexousia*) and *synergeia*, see Bonaunet 1994 b p. 5 ff.

question of whether the human being succeeds in his or her process of penance. That the belief in the possibility of succeeding in attaining our goal is a presupposition of the meaningfulness of an action is a point which G. H. von Wright has convincingly argued (cf. von Wright 1972 p. 43 f.). And Cohen's view seems then to be that our efforts of penance and reconciliation presuppose a trust in their success, which, as we have seen above, can not only be based on anthropological-psychological expectations (cf. Launay 2000 p. 84 ff.; see above p. 116 f.). Man's work of penance would, Cohen says, be meaningless without the "goal of grace", or without "die Zuversicht der Erlösung, die ihm von jenseits dieser Grenzen der Menschheit entgegenleuchtet: die Zuversicht von einem Gotte der Gnade und der Erlösung […] der die Korrelation mit dem menschlichen Individuum eingeht" (BR 67).

The relevant concept of God, Cohen states, is different from the concept of the "God of ethics": A new concept of God is demanded, corresponding to the new concept of the human being as a sinful individual (BR 62, cf. also 61, 64, 77 and 116).

> In der Ethik umstrahlt Gott die Menschheit mit der Zuversicht der Sittlichkeit auf Erden; in der Religion das Individuum mit der Zuversicht seiner persönlichen Befreiung von Schuld und Sühne, seiner Wiederherstellung zur Aufgabe der sittlichen Freiheit (BR 65).

An essential condition of this moral restoration and regeneration is precisely the reconciliation of the inner contradictions of the guilty individual and the "creation" or "Erzeugung" of the unified I, i. e. in its relation to God as sustaining the human being in its genuine or unique individuality. All this must, however, in accordance with a basic Kantian understanding of religion and the philosophy of religion, be understood in terms of the category of *hope* (RV 246).

We can not *know* whether humanity will ever attain realization as *one* universal humanity, or if the human being's actions of penance will reach their goal (RV 241), and if there will be any redemption of the individual by God.[78]

This, then, is the philosophical – ethical meaning Cohen thinks we ought to ascribe to the basic idea of monotheism, of a God who forgives sin. Further, Cohen's claim obviously is that there are no alternatives to the transition to a religious context,[79] conceivable to cope with the problems of moral guilt and redemption, and that ethics itself, therefore, requires a transition to religion. Postulating a "God of redemption" is, in his view, "a logical consequence" of the concepts of repentance and penance (BR 65), and "dass ein Gott da sei" and a correlation with God is a presupposition for the meaningfulness of the striving of the human individual for redemption from moral guilt at all (BR 64). In other words: The possibility of deciding to make a new beginning presupposes the hope of redemption. And: "Damit dieser Weg […] eingeschlagen werden kann,

---

[78] Cf. Ricoeur 1992 (1967) p. 234 f.: "It seems to me that religion is distinguished from ethics, in the fact that it requires that we think freedom under the sign of hope. […] Ethics has said all it can about evil in calling it […] a work of freedom, […] a subversion of the relation of the maxim to the law (and) […] an unfathomable disposition of freedom which makes it unavailable to itself. Religion uses another language about evil. First of all, this language places evil before God. […] This […] transforms the moral confession into a confession of sin […]. Situated before God, evil is […] in the movement of the promise: the […] beginning of […] restoration […], the initiation of a new creation".

[79] Cf. also Kant's certainty of lack of alternatives to "moral faith", as expressed in KRV: "Der Zweck ist hier unumgänglich festgestellt, und es ist nur eine einzige Bedingung nach aller meiner Einsicht möglich, unter welcher dieser Zweck […] praktische Gültigkeit habe, nämlich, dass ein Gott und eine künftige Welt sei: ich weiss auch ganz gewiss, dass niemand andere Bedingungen kenne […]. So werde ich unausbleiblich ein Dasein Gottes und ein künftiges Leben glauben, und ich bin sicher, dass diesen Glauben nichts wankend machen könnte, weil dadurch meine sittlichen Grundsätze selbst umgestürzt werden würden […]" (KRV B 856).

bedarf es des persönlichen Gottes [...] die Zuversicht auf Gott" (Schmid 2000 p. 294 f.). In this sense, then, the "God of religion" is, according to Cohen, a necessary "complementation" or "Ergänzung" for the "ethical idealization" of the human being (cf. ibid.).

I think, however, we should be content with attributing weaker validity-claims to his arguments.

First, we could note how Cohen's arguments are based, in part, on what some central *religious* ideas imply. In regard to the question if "penance" can succeed and really lead to forgiveness of guilt he asserts that: "Gott kann keine Aufgabe stellen, die nur eine Sisyphusarbeit wäre. Die Selbstheiligung muss zu dem unendlichen Abschluss kommen in der Vergebung der Sünde durch Gott" (RV 241 f.). But this is not a claim that is grounded in ethics. The ethical context generates only the idea of a hope of overcoming guilt and the moral despair involved in knowledge of one's guilt. Concerning whether the idea of God's forgiveness would be incompatible with human autonomy, Cohen asserts that if we assign all tasks to man, and none to God, then the religious correlation between man and God would collapse ("denn [...] würde das Grundgerüst der religiösen Erkenntnis, das wir in der Korrelation von Mensch und Gott errichtet haben, zusammenbrechen" (RV 242)). But here the explicit concern is what is required in order that religion, and not ethics, should be meaningful. And the argument does not focus on the question of how ethics leads to religion.

In accordance with this emphasis on the task of giving philosophical – ethical meaning to the contents of religion, we can read parts of Cohen's philosophy of religion as a philosophical theology, rather than as contributions to a transcendental philosophical justification of religion. Cohen's concern in this respect is a search for an understanding of the concept of God in relation to the human being as an individual, which grows out of Jewish prophetism and the Psalms. Further, he seeks to articulate a doctrine of God's attributes in which he explicitly builds on mediaeval philosophical theology, making special reference to Maimonides. God's (thirteen!) attributes must, according to Cohen's reading of Maimonides, be understood in terms of ethical action (cf. RV 251). Any other attributes are, Cohen asserts, of no significance for an understanding of the concept of God of monotheism. The thought of the recognition of and liberation from guilt gives Cohen the opportunity for a philosophical-theological exposition of "goodness" as one of God's essential attributes, i.e. precisely in terms of forgiveness of sin (cf. RV 242f., 246f. and 249). "Goodness" which reveals itself in forgiveness of sin, and "holiness", which Cohen conceives as connected to the "moral law" as a Divine commandment, are according to Cohen the basic attributes that must be ascribed to God within an adequate philosophical theology (cf. RV 243f. and 249f.).[80]

But now, concerning the claim of how ethics leads to religion, I think we can admit its validity only in a weaker sense than Cohen himself seems to assert. We can see a transition to a religious dimension as giving meaning to a hope of overcoming moral guilt and despair, and to a moral regeneration. According to Cohen, the longing for redemption is an expression of a natural human predisposition to overcome despair: "die Sehnsucht nach Erlösung [...] entspricht dem Naturtriebe des Menschen, nicht an sich selbst zu verzweifeln, [...] um nicht [...] zugrunde zu gehen" (RV 435f.). And

---

[80] Cohen does not address the problem of how we should conceive God's forgiveness of sin as effecting a *removal* of guilt (cf. Adams 1997 p. xv). This question is left without any complete solution also in Kant's philosophy of religion (cf. Wimmer 1990 § 15). Solving this problem is however hardly a necessary presupposition for rational faith in the possibility of redemption or liberation from guilt in virtue of God's goodness, which manifests itself in forgiveness of sin. Cf. Kant's words: "[...] fürs Vernünfteln ist es ein unerreichbares Geheimnis" (Rel. B 216). But I think we should follow Kant in allowing the existence of "mysteries" ("Geheimnisse") within a moral rational faith (cf. Wimmer 1990 p. 167).

corresponding to this: "In dem Verlangen nach Gott besteht die Religion. In dem Verlangen nach einem Wesen *ausser dem Menschen*, aber *für den Menschen* besteht sie" (BR 138).

Cohen's view, as we have seen, is that we must resign before the task of accounting for the possibility of reconciliation within the limits of our merely anthropological existence (cf. Cohen's question: "Wie konnte dies aber menschlich gedacht werden [...]?" (RV 246); see above p. 119). But we cannot *apriori* exclude the possibility of alternative, non-religious languages, practices and ontologies supporting our search for sense in the face of moral despair. And further, of course, we have no rationally justified certainty that the human existence is not, in this respect – and others – basically tragic, and that N. Hartmann is right in his statement that the human being has to bear his or her guilt, even if this would lead to the ruin of one's life.[81] (We can, however, see the relevance of asserting that an attitude like this would be in contradiction to the claims of morality itself.)

Thus, if we admit that Cohen has shown that the problem of moral guilt can meaningfully be understood within – if not necessarily exclusively within – a religious context, as I think we should, (in spite of the fact that some questions on the possibility of a philosophically articulated conception of moral regeneration and of the relation between human and Divine contributions in this process might seem to be lacking completely clear answers, both in Cohen and in the history of philosphy and theology in general), we can accept his thought on these matters as a contribution to a rational justification of a religious form of life, as a "continuation" of and as "completing" the ethical conception of man, even if we will reject a

---

[81] One might also want to reject the entire problem complex of moral guilt. But this rejection, at the same time, would imply a rejection of the ethical dimension of the human existence altogether, insofar as the problem of guilt seems to be intrinsically connected with ethics (cf. above p. 73 ff.).

claim that we here have compelling arguments for a transition from ethics to religion. We might perhaps argue that an interpretation in terms of religion is the one giving the best account (so far) of phenomena in human existence such as repentance and redemption from moral guilt, or at least, that it gives *a* reasonable account. For a contribution to a justification of religion and of its "participation in (ethical) reason", it would be sufficient to show how a religious discourse opens for us a meaningful and relevant way of facing the problems of moral guilt. We could say, then, that this would be a contribution to a justification of the legitimacy of religion as an account of its "intelligibility" (cf. Schillebeeckx 1994 p. 56).

This interpretation of the idea of a transition from ethics to religion comes, I think, very close to M. Scheler's conception of how repentance (Reue), which according to Scheler is the essential element in man's strivings towards moral regeneration (cf. above p. 105 ff.), "assumes its full meaning and becomes, as it were, fully articulate" by being incorporated into, and experienced within, "the universal framework of metaphysics and religion", and where repentance is understood "as the mysterious process known as 'forgiveness of sin'" ("den geheimnisreichen Vorgang 'Vergebung der Sünde'") and "as an infusion of new strength": "(eine) Eingiessung einer neuen Kraft aus dem Zentrum der Dinge", as a "grace" (VEM 50). According to Scheler, transcending our mere humanity, towards "ein geahntes Zentrum der Dinge, in aller Dinge ewige Kraftquelle" (VEM 51) ", in an intentional movement "in eine unsichtbare Sphäre hinein", of which we are seeking to grasp the "mysterious outlines" in the concept of "an eternal and infinite judge, an eternal and infinite mercy, an infinite might, an eternal source of life", belongs to the immanent meaning of repentance experienced in full measure (cf. Scheler VEM p. 52 ff.). This conception, according to which an interpretation in terms of a religious context is what gives the best account of the phenomena of redemption from moral guilt, I understand as a central piece of Kantian reflection of philosophy of religion, within

Scheler's otherwise anti-Kantian rhetorics. And this is also the interpretation that I think best grasps the essence of Cohen's thought of a transition from ethics to a religious attitude, in connection with the problems of self-knowledge of and redemption from moral guilt.

It is not the case then that morality leads to religion in the sense that there are compelling philosophical arguments for entering the religious dimension: Cohen has not proven that there is any necessity of transcending the boundary where ethics meets religion. As H. O. Ollig correctly states, his arguments do not have the strength of making "die Aufnahme des Glaubens logisch zwingend", and they have not established any "Nötigung des Redens von Gott" (cf. Ollig 1979 p. 340 and 341). But providing such arguments is not the task of philosophical reflection and justification either. Questions concerning our fundamental attitudes towards our human existence cannot be solved within any philosophical (or theological) thinking (cf. Wimmer 1990 p. 10). Rather, the criterion is what proves to be of lasting value in the life of a human being. Even if it is hard to spell out in detail, F. von Kutschera's concept of "Bewährung im Leben" as the fundamental criterion of religion and the philosophy of religion (Kutschera 1991 p. 242),[82] is, I think, in some sense basically true. Correspondingly, our fundamental attitudes have their ground in our experience of our human existence itself: "Life can educate one to a belief in God. And *experiences* too are what bring this about; but I don't mean visions and other forms of sense experience which

---

82 Cf. also M. Buber: "The meaning that has been received can be proved true by each man only in the singleness of his being and the singleness of his life" (here after Seeskin 1990 p. 106). With regard to the limits of philosophy in relation to religion, Buber correspondingly asserts that "the most philosophy can do is to *point* to God. Philosophy [...] recognizes its inherent limitations and moves out of the way" (ibid. p. 108). A similar conception is expressed also in V. Lossky (1978 chapter I; see also Bonaunet 1993 p. 507 ff.).

show us the "existence of this being", but, e.g. sufferings of various sorts. [...] Experiences, thoughts, – life can force this concept on us" (Wittgenstein CV 86e). And as H. Holzey states: "Umkehr [...] lässt sich philosophisch nicht rechtfertigen, sie liegt als biografisches Faktum philosophischer Sinngebung voraus" (Holzhey 2000 p. 40). In this sense, the reflection of the philosopher of religion is always secondary, but unavoidable for the religious philosopher since it belongs to the unavoidable project of *fides quaerens intellectum*, and also unavoidable for the philosopher seeking to understand the faith of others.

It might be objected against a traditional Kantian philosophy of religion, and Cohen's, that its basis for the account of the ground of the legitimacy and intelligibility of religion is too narrow, i.e. insofar as this basis is the "moral point of view" in a Kantian sense. Cohen's reflections within his philosophy of religion indeed includes various aspects of the human condition, and contains insights concerning human weakness, poverty, misery and suffering (cf. Löwith 1968 p. 375). Still, the moral claims in relation to the fellow human being, and especially my transgressions of these claims and the problems of knowledge and forgiveness of guilt, are the primary objects of Cohen's attention. Against a conception of this kind, P. Tillich asserts that the question of forgiveness of guilt or sin is not a central concern for modern man (cf. Tillich ST I p. 49). For Tillich, the problem is the existential situation of the human being in a much wider sense: The existential conditions of the modern human being in a state of alienation from its essential nature, as a state characterized of dehumanization, reification ("man becomes a thing and ceases to be a person"), threatened by lack of meaning and filled with anxiety (ST II s. 25), the anxiety of "not-being" or of having to die (cf. ibid. p. 66f.). "The state of existence is the state of estrangement. Man is estranged from the ground of his being, from other beings and from himself" (ibid. p. 44), or "from [...] God, one's self, one's world" (ibid. p. 46). And it is in relation to these concerns that man strives towards and longs for "reconciliation": "It is the question of a reality in which the self-estrangement of our existence is overcome, a reality of reconciliation and reunion, [...] meaning and hope" (ST I p. 49). Kant's and Cohen's concentration on the dimension of morality, might then seem to represent a perspective which is too restricted and too narrow for us who live under the threath of "existential despair" and "the threat of nihilism as expressed in twentieth century literature, art, and psychology" (ST II p. 16). Corresponding to this, it might then also be objected that the approach of a Kantian philosophy of religion to the problem of a justification of participating in the practices and institutions, lacks relevance or is of restricted importance in our times.

We should, I think, concede a point to Tillich, because he refers to additional potentials of a – in a wide sense – Kantian philosophy of religion. The concern of Tillich's project, especially in the second volume of his "Systematic Theology", is also in a certain sense the transition from ethics to religion, however ethics is here conceived in a more comprehensive sense, as including the problems of the meaning of the human existence.[83] But the structure of Tillich's thinking in ST II is in my view definitely "Kantian", insofar as Tillich seeks to articulate questions which are implicit in the human (ethical) existence, and then to suggest answers grounded in religious traditions, in order to contribute to making these intelligible. Here he also reveals, I think, his direct dependence on Cohen, and proceeds according to what he designates a "method of correlation" in which existential questions and theological answers are explicated in mutual dependence or "correlation" to each other. The basis for the legitimacy of this method is finally "the divine – human relation" itself as a "correlation" (ST I p. 61): "[...] human existence itself is the question" (ibid. p. 65).

---

83 An approach of this kind, i. e. as based in the existential problems of meaning, can not be characterized as "eudaimonistic" in the sense which Cohen rejects.

"Man is the question he asks about himself, before any question has been formulated" (ibid. p. 62). And: "God is the answer to the question implied in human finitude" (ibid. p. 64).

But it must be conceded that (transgressions of) morality represents a core idea also with respect to the existentialist analysis of the human being's alienation from the essentially human, as in Tillich, and as an inescapable aspect of phenomena such as dehumanization and reification. And moral guilt, according to Kant's and Cohen's understanding, clearly contains elements of "alienation" insofar as morality, in the Kantian sense, most deeply and essentially concerns how I relate myself to the Other(s) and to myself. We also should note how Tillich himself emphasizes that the concept of "alienation" ought not to replace the concept of sin. For "sin" expresses the "personal" character of the alienation which belongs to the existential situation of the human being, because the personal act of sin highlights the individual's freedom as well as his/her personal responsibility and guilt.[84] "Man's predicament is estrangement, but his estrangement is sin" (ST II p. 46).

In light of this, Tillich's remark finding the narrow focus on the concept of sin constrained and restricted because of "the reference [...] to the existential conflicts of Jewish legalism" (ST II p. 16) doesn't necessarily strike at Cohen, or diminish the import of a "Cohenian" philosophy of religion. Earlier, with Cohen's insights as our basis, supported by Hartmann, Scheler and a bit by Ricoeur, we have realized the importance and unavoidability of a philosophically – ethically formulated and justified concept of moral guilt.

---

84 – even if the human existential situation and the human agent, as Tillich emphasizes, ought not to be understood exclusively in personal categories and under the idea of freedom, but also as subject to the conditions of "destiny" (cf. e.g. ST II p. 31 ff.), or as, according to W. Kamlah's appropriate wording, in the field of the tension between "Handlung und Widerfahrnis" (cf. Kamlah 1973 p. 34 ff.).

Cohen's project of a philosophy of religion, then, is based on a fundamental problem of the human existential situation.

If we now look at this from the perspective of religion, we also realize how precisely Cohen emphasizes the problem of guilt as an essential basis for a philosophical approach to religion. Because guilt is one of the most problematical aspects of the human existence, the problem of guilt, as several philosophers and historians of religion have demonstrated within the phenomenology of religion, also is of central importance for religion – "from animism to Zen" (cf. Westphal 1984 p. 74, cf. also p. 114).[85]

5. Cohen and the autonomy of religion

1. Cohen's conception, as we have seen earlier, is that human practical individuality can only be adequately understood within the context of religion, and more specifically, in terms of a correlation "unique individual" – "unique God": "Der religiöse Mensch ist schlechthin Individuum. Und diese Individualität wird ihm von der

---

[85] Cf. also Ricoeur who states just this point by his remark that: "Some decades ago, Professor Petazzoni [...] wrote a collection of works covering the entire field of comparative religions. He called this precisely *Confession of Sins*" (Ricoeur 1992 (1967) p. 224). Within the context of the phenomenology of religion, G. Widengren points out the importance of confession of sin and penance within e.g. Babylonian religion, Zoroastrism, Vedic religion, Jainism and Buddhism, referring also to examples from China, Japan, Asia Minor, South Arabia and America. Nonetheless he simultaneously indicates how the concepts of sin and penance are of "sensationally little importance" ("uppseendeväckande ringa roll") within Indo-European religions, outside Indo-Iranian culture, and also in Islam (see Widengren 1971 chapter 8).

Korrelation mit Gott verliehen" (BR 92). The Other is constituted as a concrete *you* before me through my attitude of *Mitleid* towards him/her. My I-identity is strengthened already by this, i.e. because *I* accept responsibility in relation to the suffering of the Other. But according to Cohen, this relation between me and the Other can only be made manifest in its complete meaning insofar as the I–you correlation is placed under a correlation to God as the one who has unconditional love towards the human individual. My individuality is further consolidated when I acknowledge my own guilt for the suffering of the Other whom I have offended. A reconciliation and restoration of relationship with the Other, and a healing of my inner dividedness, presupposes according to Cohen, that I am placing myself in correlation to a transcendent Being, God, who finally guarantees that my work of penance will succeed.

But then, as H. Holzhey remarks: "[...] wenn Gott in dieser Relation mehr als eine nützliche Funktion sein soll, muss ich ihm vernünftigerweise als einzigen, schaffenden und selbständig gegen mich handelnden Gott denken" (Holzhey 2000 p. 42). This is, however, a disputed point in interpreting Cohen. According to M. Buber's criticism of Cohen, it remains unsettled whether Cohen ever gets beyond a Kantian conception of God as an "idea of reason" and as a regulative principle. In ERW, the concept of God is understood in terms of an idea which is a necessary condition for establishing unity between nature and morality within Cohen's system of philosophy (cf. Buber 1952 p. 54). Further, Buber interprets Cohen's development in understanding the concept of God as a psychological – biographical struggle in which "Cohen, the thinker, defends himself against the belief which, rising out of an ancient heritage, threatens to overwhelm him. He defends himself with success: the success of the system-creator. Cohen has constructed the last home for the God of the philosophers" (ibid.). And even if Cohen's own religious experience shows itself in his later works through various formulations of God' love as the "cornerstone" of (Jewish) religion,

Cohen maintains, Buber asserts, at the level of the principles of the philosophy of religion, that God must be conceived as an abstract idea and an ethical ideal (cf. ibid. p. 55). In one sense, Buber seems to accept Rosenzweig's view that Cohen's idea of God should not be understood as meaning that God, for Cohen, remains "a mere idea", but, again, as being only of biographical – psychological import: "[…] I permit myself to say that though Cohen indeed thought of God as an idea, Cohen, too, loved him as – God" (ibid. p. 58).

To be sure, Cohen talks about God as idea and ethical ideal (cf. RV 185 ff.). But he does not conceive of this exclusively in terms of Kantian ideas of reason and, more specifically, of God only as a regulative idea of ethical reason, and as a thought we must postulate to understand ourselves as moral beings and to be able to meaningfully strive for moral perfection (cf. Röd 1999 p. 39). God is, at least, according to Cohen, as K. Seeskin points out (referring to E. Fackenheim's criticism of Cohen), an idea more in the way that The Idea of the Good by Plato is idea, i.e. as an eternal, transcendent principle (cf. Seeskin 1990 p. 104). This, in itself, is already important, because it refutes that God as idea could be philosophically conceived as immanent to the human consciousness only, as a "thought" or "only as a moral relation in me" (cf. Kant in Opus Postumum, here after Buber 1952 p. 51). In this regard we should note Cohen's statement in BR that:

> Die Erkenntnis […] setzt sich selbst die Grundlegung des Seins, als einer Realität, die nicht innerhalb des Bewusstseins selbst gelegen und beschränkt sei. Für alles Sein der Erkenntnis errichtet sich diese selbst die Grundlegung der Absolutheit, der Transzendenz (BR 137).[86]

---

86 Cf. M. Dreyer's formulation of Cohen's position: The human being as religious subject is defined "durch das Bewusstsein, sich einem Wesen zu verdanken, das, ausserhalb von ihm, tranzendent zu Natur und Menschenwelt, ihn geschaffen hat, seine Gattung erhält und ihn von seiner Schuld befreit" (Dreyer 1985 p. 217).

Now Seeskin also argues that, for Cohen, God is not the One who *is*, but the One who acts (Seeskin 1990 p. 15), and that Cohen takes God out of ontology and locates him instead within the normative dimension (cf. below p. 137). But as *Sein* in relation to *Dasein*, and as "ground of being", Cohen's idea of God cannot, I think, be deprived of ontological relevance. (I will say more on this below.)

But God, according to Cohen's explicit statement, is also idea and ideal: The human being's love of God is love of an idea and "the ethical ideal". "Nur das Ideal kann ich lieben, und das Ideal kann ich nicht anders fassen, es sei denn, dass ich es liebe. Das Ideal ist das Urbild der Sittlichkeit" (RV 187). To the question of how it is possible to love an idea, Cohen replies by means of a a counter-question: "Wie kann man etwas anderes lieben als eine Idee?" (RV 185). Buber rejects all of this. Seeskin pertinently summarizes Buber's criticism: "According to Buber, one cannot love an idea and certainly one cannot be loved by one. The relation of loving and being loved are irreducibly personal. 'God loves as a personality and [...] wishes to be loved like a personality' [...] (Buber)" (Seeskin 1990 p. 109). – Seeskin's strategy in relation to Buber's Cohen-critique seems to be to demonstrate how Buber's ascription of personality to God and Cohen's understanding of God as idea are convergent, insofar as "personality" also essentially involves a normative or ideal element. "[...] by its very nature, love is normative [...]" (ibid. p. 111). And, in particular, with respect to the love of God:

> By loving God, I love someone who wills the moral law. [...]. [...] then to respond to Him as a person, I have [...] to will it myself [...]. If this is what one means by a personal God, no one was more committed to this belief than Cohen. Insofar as personality is a normative concept and concerns what ought to be, God is the personality *par excellence* (ibid. p. 115).

Cohen's statement concerning God as idea could then be understood as an insistence on the unavoidability of the normative – ideal dimension of the concept of God, in connection with the limitations with regard to what we can know as belonging to the essence of God, in accordance with a negative – theological fundamental conception (cf. above p. 30). This seems reasonable, as far as it goes. But in my opinion, Cohen would hardly assert in his later works that God, as *Sein*, is *identical* with a moral ideal, implying that his Being (Sein) is entirely grasped in terms of "the One who gives the moral law". God is "Sein" or Being itself. And God as "Sein" transcends any idea of reason.

2. A fundamental thought in H. Scholz's philosophy of religion is that the basic criterion "an dem man die Religion überhaupt erkennen [...] kann [...] ist das Gottesbewusstsein" (Scholz 1922 p. 16). "Consciousness of God" is, in other words, the peculiar category of religion (cf. ibid. p. 18), and what characterizes religion as a *phaenomenon sui generis* (cf. ibid. p. 18 and 29 f.). – Insofar as I can see Cohen's conception is in accordance with this. Cohen thus asserts that: "Für alle Entwicklung der Religion [...] muss der Begriff des einzigen Gottes der unveränderliche Schwerpunkt bleiben" (BR 120). Similarly, in reference to his account of hope and trust as basic forms of religious faith, he says that these also are affects that belong to the common human consciousness, but that what constitutes them *qua* religious is that God is their intentional object ("Zielpunkt") (cf. BR 101). Religious faith in all its aspects, whether connected with compassion or *Mitleid* with the Other and the problem of my guilt, according to Cohen's philosophy of religion, is essentially directed towards God as acting and the One who has mercy.

3. "In dem Verlangen nach Gott besteht die Religion. In dem Verlangen nach einem Wesen *ausser dem Menschen*, aber *für den Menschen* besteht sie" (BR 138). And more precisely: "Der Mensch und Gott, Gott und der Mensch, in dieser Doppelfügung vollzieht sich das religiöse Bewusstsein" (BR 90). Neither God alone nor the hu-

man being alone constitutes the contents of the religious consciousness, but the human being, i.e. the individual, in correlation with God (cf. BR 97). From what we could designate as Cohen's basic conception of a phenomenology of religion, the distinctive character of religion appears as concentrated in the concept of correlation. The correlation is reciprocal: Not God alone and in Himself, but always in correlation to the human being, and never the human being alone, but always in correlation to God. At the same time, there is an insurmountable distance between the two parts of the correlation. There is no equality of status between them:

> Die Korrelation ist nicht schlechthin Wechselverhältnis, sondern Gott wird ihr Schwerpunkt. In diesen Schwerpunkt wird das Sein verlegt. [...] als dieser Schwerpunkt trägt Gott einzig das Sein. Der Natur und dem Menschen gegenüber ist er [...] der Einzige (BR 137).

Finally, the "uniqueness" (*"Einzigkeit"*) of the human individual is not equal to the "uniqueness" or *"Einzigkeit"* of God (cf. Wiehl 2000 p. 408).[87] Thus, there is an asymmetry within the correlation, in which God is the foundation and presupposition (cf. Löwith 1968 p. 365f.), and not man: "Gott entsteht, er erzeugt sich in diesem Bunde mit dem Menschen. Sein Ursprung ist der Bund mit dem Menschen"[88]. Yet: "Dieser Bund ist das Kunstwerk Gottes, [...] nicht [...] des Menschen" (BR 96). It is beyond doubt that Cohen, in vir-

---

87   In RV, Cohen indicates this at one point by distinguishing between God's "Einzigkeit" and the human being's "eigene Einheit" (cf. RV 38), while in BR he always characterizes the correlation God – man in terms of "einziger Gott" / "einziger Mensch" (BR 61 f.).

88   Cf. P. Tillich: "[...] although God in his abysmal nature is in no way dependent on man, God in his self-manifestation to man is dependent on the way man receives his manifestation" (Tillich ST I p. 61). "There is a mutual interdependence between 'God for us' and 'we for God'" (ibid.).

tue of the concept of the correlation between God and man as a basic concept in his philosophy of religion, transcends Kant's conception. Further, the correlation is not a correlation between concepts or "mere ideas", but it implies an ontological dimension, where God as *Sein* is the foundation.

This thought, i. e. of God as *Sein*, and therefore as incommensurable with all existence, also is sufficient to secure a fundamental aspect of God's radical "otherness" or "die Abgründigkeit Gottes" (Ollig 1979 a p. 344). K. Seeskin connects this, as we already suggested above, to an understanding of God as a regulative idea. As a regulative idea, God is not something that exists like other objects exist. "He remains radically "other" – an "otherness that Cohen captures by taking God out of the realm of the ontological and putting him in the realm of the normative" (Seeskin 1990 p. 102). I cannot agree, however, with Seeskin in this, and God's "otherness" can in my view in important respects be conceived already in terms of God as *Sein* (cf. above).

Whether there is an ontological dimension in Cohen's thought is, as is well known, disputed. Concerning this discussion, M. Heidegger's criticism has been very influential. According to Heidegger's criticism, Cohen rejected any ontological – metaphysical commitments, both in his interpretations of Kant and in his own philosophical system (cf. Holzhey 1994 p. 17). But this question is controversial also with regard to Cohen's late philosophy. Cohen himself states, as Seeskin notes, in RV that the place of being is taken by action: "An die Stelle des Seins tritt sonach die Handlung" (RV 109). This could be interpreted to imply that Cohen (still) rejects ontology, at least in its traditional sense. On the other hand, it is obvious that securing a connection between what he designates as "logic" and religion is a main concern for Cohen in his two last works in the philosophy of religion. The decisive moment in this regard is the concept of "God's Being" or *Sein*. Through this Cohen connects, as we have suggested above (p. 29) his own conception with the ontological thinking of Eleatic and Platonic philosophy. This does not commit him, however, to an Aristotelian-Scholastic metaphysics of substances, nor to an "objectivating" perspective with regard to God (cf. Wimmer 1992 p. 97 f.), as a substance possessing attributes. On the other hand, neither is a connection to a metaphysics of this kind any criterion for ascribing an ontological dimension to Cohen's thought.

At least, I find it difficult to understand Cohen's statement that the place of being is taken by action (cf. above) implying a "suspension" of the ontological, i. e. so that God's *Sein* and *Einzigkeit* would be reduced to (the being of) a normative ideal, or, in other words, that the "logical" and ontological dimension should be reduced to ethical ideality. The emphasis on God's *Sein* and uniqueness in relation to all *Dasein* and "becoming" (*Werden*), and the "ontological difference" Cohen thereby articulates (cf. R. Wiehl, see above note 18), constitutes, as far as I can see, an irreducible ontological perspective in his thinking. Corresponding to this God is, for Cohen, the Unlimited in relation to all spatial and temporal limitedness, the "Urground" and the ground of the possibility of all movement, and the Eternal in relation to all change (RV 52 f.; cf. Ollig 1978 p. 369 and 1979 a p. 348).

It is, however, a problem in Cohen's approach, according to H. O. Ollig, that he poses such metaphysical statements on God besides the ethical, and thus operates with a "duality" of statements concerning God (Ollig 1979 a p. 348), but in a way that implies an unmediated juxtaposition of ontological and ethical predicates (ibid. p. 347). But in my opinion we neither have to reject the presence of a genuine ontological dimension in Cohen's philosophy of religion, nor to accept Ollig's criticism of an unmediated juxtaposition. Rather than understanding Cohen as asserting that action ought to *replace* being with regard to the conception of God, we could direct our attention to his statement that: "das metaphysische Problem von Sein und Werden *hinüberzuleiten* geeignet ist auf das ethische Problem, welches von sich aus eine Verbindung herzustellen suchen muss zwischen dem einzigen Sein und dem endlichen Werden" (RV 80; ital. KB). We find a clue to an adequate understanding of this "transition" or *Hinüberleitung*, in Ollig's remark on how God's *Sein* as uniqueness and incomparability ("Unvergleichbarkeit") (RV 51) in Cohen should be conceived of in terms of a (Jewish) negative theology (cf. Ollig 1978 p. 368): When the "center of gravity" with regard to Cohen's concept of God lies in the ethical predicates, while the ontological predicates are thematized only more sporadically, this is due precisely to a central idea of negative theology, i.e. that God cannot be thematized "directly" in his essence, but only indirectly by his "energies", or as Cohen says, "effects" ("Wirkungen") (cf. RV 93 and 110), through "attributes of action", creation, revelation and redemption, (cf. Ollig 1979 a p. 335). Cohen states explicitly that the metaphysical attributes are "negative attributes" (RV 47 and 53; cf. also RV 70 ff.), and that "the uniqueness of God's *Sein*" represents only a "negative determination", which requires a "positive value" (RV 68) and through this a relation or connection between "unique Being" and the "existence" of "becoming" (RV 80, cf. also 68 and 70), i.e. in the final instance in terms of the determination of "God's ethical meaning" (RV 53). But this does not mean that the ontological dimension in the "metaphysics of monotheism" (RV 54) ought to be annihilated, or that the "metaphysical point of view", "der vom Problem des Seins beherrscht wird" (RV 79), should be replaced by the ethical. On the contrary, I think that the ontological dimension should be preserved as a necessary foundation of our relating to God through the ethical, preventing God from being conceived of only as "a moral relation in me" with the result that religion, again, would be reduced to ethics, and also that this represents a possible and reasonable reading of Cohen.

4. Cohen's general concern in his philosophy of religion is to establish a *Rechtsgrund*, or a "ground" of the legitimacy of religion, by reconstructing core elements of a "religion of reason" and demon-

strating their connection (primarily) to ethics as a "doctrine of the human being". In this way he wanted to show how religion contributes some peculiar contents which complement ethics. The contents which are articulated constitute, however, in a certain sense only, as we could say, certain minimum contents of religion.[89] The basic idea is the consciousness of God, or to be more precise: The correlation God – human individual. This is, as we have seen, in Cohen's late philosophy characteristically interpreted in connection to the problems of compassion and guilt. It is essential that the contents of religion must be the contents which are required by the problems which have their origin in ethics. Further, any legitimate religions must, as Cohen expressed it, be in "homogenity" with the claims implied by ethics: The correlation between God and the human being ought to be reflected, therefore, in the correlation between human beings as *Mensch* and *Mitmensch*: The human individual's love of God must be mediated through his love of the fellow human being, and only in this correlation does the meaning of the superior correlation become realized (cf. Löwith 1968 p. 367): "Die Korrelation von Mensch und Gott ist in erster Linie die vom Menschen, als Mitmenschen, zu Gott" (RV 133). Correspondingly, guilt-consciousness must motivate one to abolish the "social sins" within human reality: From the knowledge of guilt the individual is led, through the hope of redemption by God, out of his resignation towards renewed efforts to overcome social injustice and suffering by moral respect and compassion (cf. Schmid 2000 p. 298).

As we have emphasized above (p. 11) the contents of a "religion of reason" are not to be conceived of as generated by a philo-

---

89 Thus I accept, in a certain sense, H. L. Ollig's remark that there is a phenomenological "Defizit" in Cohen (cf. Ollig 1979 a p. 341 f.). But neither is it the aim of Cohen's philosophy of religion "die religiöse Phänomenalität immanent aus sich auszulegen" (cf. ibid.).

sophical – ethical reason. A basic thought held both by Kant and Cohen was that ethics *leads to* religion. P. Byrne states:

> If reflection on moral concepts leads to the necessity of making use of religious concepts [...] the content of those religious concepts must be other than purely moral. If the content of religious concepts is purely moral, then morality has not led anywhere: no route from morality to religion has been established. [...] In order for a Kantian-style project in the philosophy of religion to succeed, *something* must be borrowed from the concept of the divine rooted in history and/or metaphysics. Only with such a borrowing can independent sense be given to the notion of the divine so as to give something for morality to lead to (Byrne 1998 p. 5 f.).

In accordance with this understanding, it belongs to Cohen's agenda already in ERW that philosophical ethics, without prejudices, must turn towards religious tradition and its talk of God (cf. ERW 432; see Holzhey 2000 p. 53).

The contents of religion can not, then, be "deduced" from ethics. The main point of connection between religion and philosophical reason is the ethical. Religion must, as Cohen points out repeatedly, remain closely and continuously connected with ethics (cf. e.g. RV 195 f. and 215). Contents that are of immediate ethical relevance must, therefore, also constitute the core of religion according to a Kantian understanding of religion. This does not imply, however, that the contents of religion therefore ought to be reduced to ethics. "Trans-rational" and "trans-ethical" contents can also be admitted according to an understanding like this. Insofar as ethics *leads to* religion (cf. above), what matters is transcending the realm of ethics, but the "trans-rational" and "trans-ethical" must essentially preserve an unbroken continuity with ethics.

For that reason Cohen can understand as belonging to the peculiarity of the religious consciousness (cf. BR 107), as a "particular" ("eigentümliche") form of consciousness, longing, faith, trust in God by "the praying I", for "rescue and redemption through Him" (cf. BR 104 f.). And as a continuation of this, we find in Cohen's philosophy of religion extended hermeneutic expositions of religious rituals connected to the longing for redemption, as in RV, chapter XII, on the "Day of Atonement"), and of prayer in RV, chapter XVII, where the correlation between "sinful individual" and "redeeming God" is experienced, and which gives "consolation to the suffering individual" (cf. Schmid 2000 p. 295). Thus prayer constitutes, according to Cohen, "die Grundkraft der religiösen Idealisierung, welche die Welt der Gemeinschaft von Gott und Mensch, welche die Korrelation fordert, stets vom neuem hervorbringt und befestigt" (RV 463).

It is, however, reasonable to admit that there are some limitations to Cohen's exposition of the contents of religion and especially the concept of God. These limitations, however, can be understood, in part, as a reflection of his preference of a negative theology, and therefore as appropriate to the same degree as negative theology is a viable position. A tendency towards an alliance with an apophatic theology is characteristic of the entire Kantian tradition of the philosophy of religion (cf. Byrne 1998 p. 7; see also Seeskin 1990 p. 56 ff.). K. Löwith proposes that the meaning of Cohen's thought of God as idea ought to be interpreted precisely in terms of a negative theology:

"Gott ist Idee" besagt negativ: er ist weder ein Ding noch eine leibhafte Person noch ein personifizierter höchster Begriff. Sogar das Attribut der Lebendigkeit, sagt Cohen in Übereinstimmumg mit Maimonides, könne ihm nicht zugesprochen werden. Auch kein Dasein im Sinne von Existenz [...]. [...] Man kann Gott weder beschreiben und darstellen noch begreifen (Löwith 1968 p. 360).

The thought of God as *Sein* might, I think, be interpreted in a similar way.

5. As R. Wiehl emphasizes, Cohen's philosophical efforts, in general, and his philosophy of religion are quite close to Kant's philosophy. His concern is an incessant "Philosophieren mit Kant", because Kant's philosophy for Cohen was the true philosophy, and an ex-

pression of the living reality of the human culture of *Humanität*. And: "Nur eine Weiterentwicklung, eine Fortbildung dieser Wahrheit konnte es geben" (Wiehl 1998 p. 153). Kant's statement that he, by his critique of reason, has restricted the realm of our knowledge to make place for faith (cf. above p. 10) is also true of Cohen. But as Wiehl further points out:

> Der hier nun eröffnete Raum für den Vernunftglauben war wesentlich weiter ausgebreitet, weit über den Bereich einer philosophischen Ethik hinaus: es war der Raum für einen neuen Vernunftglauben, welches an die Schöpfung der Welt, an die Offenbarung Gottes in der Welt und an die Erlösung des Menschen [...] glaubt (Wiehl 1998 p. 166).

The transcendental philosophical approach to religion is then concentrated on what serves man's ethical idealization. However, that does not mean that the contents of religion are confined to this, insofar as a negative theology, as Cohen's, admits an approach towards God through God's "energies".

Cohen's philosophy of religion does not, in spite of its essential connection to ethics, imply any "functionalistic leveling" of religion (cf. Ollig 1979 a. p. 342). On the other hand, Cohen also avoids recourse to understanding religion exclusively in terms of a religious experience only open to special access through faith (cf. ibid.), even if Cohen also accepts and explicitly talks about an access of this kind (see below).

6. A justification of the truth of religion cannot be the purpose of (Kantian) philosophy of religion and its project of showing the legitimacy of religion. Indeed, the reflection of the philosophy of religion should aim at an assessment and decisions concerning relevant validity claims. But the object of this decision cannot be the truth of religion. This object, rather, must be the rational "possibility of religion" ("Möglichkeit von Religiosität" (cf. Haeffner 1997 p. 183, 185 and 193; see also Scholz 1922 p. 284 and 304 ff.)). Philosophy

of religion can and ought to articulate negative criteria for the possible truth of (a) religion, as primarily ethical criteria (cf. Haeffner 1997 p. 186f. and 195) (cf. also above p. 70). But positive criteria must, as G. Haeffner points out, in the final instance, be of an immanent – religious character (cf. ibid. p. 187): "Der religiöse Glaube bezieht sich [...] auf Erfahrungstatsachen einer eigenen Ordnung" (ibid. p. 191).[90] In Cohen we find the thought that religious consciousness has its own peculiar certainty which transcends a certainty grounded in "practical indispensability" and "inner feeling of obligation" (Cohen *versus* E. Troeltsch, BR 94). In this respect, "real" or "true" religion remains closed to philosophical reason, as this does not have genuine access to the foundations of religion (cf. Holzhey 2000 p. 38). This does not, however, imply that religious consciousness is closed to philosophical critique, insofar as it ought to meet the negative criteria for the possible truth of religious faith, and further the requirement of critical reason of intelligibility. These are the functions of a Kantian philosophy of religion as Cohen's, insofar as it provides a contribution to an understanding of the ground of the legitimacy or *Rechtsgrund* of this peculiar religious consciousness, warranting the possibility of a rational belief in the possibility of religion, precisely by an explanation of its "intelligibility" (cf. above p. 126), through a demonstration of its continuity or homogenity with the ethical dimension in the human existence. – And this seems to be the limit of a *philosophy* of religion. I don't think that this implies falling back into precritical dogmatism. Denying the legitimacy of a genuine religious consciousness, not fully transparent to philosophical reason, would however, I think, imply not recognizing the

---

90 Cf. P. Tillich: "[...] there is no having the content of faith except in the act of faith [...] because that which is meant in the act of faith cannot be approached in any other way than through an act of faith" (DF p. 10f.). Tillich talks in this connection of a "correlation of faith" as a "correlation between the subject and object of faith" (cf. ibid. p. 59).

limits of (philosophical) rationality, and, it seems to me, risk falling into an absolute or "dogmatic" rationalism, as distinguished from a critical philosophy, recognizing also its own limitations.

In this sense Cohen's reflections on the philosophy of religion meet, I think, the demands we made at the beginning, of an acceptable or viable Kantian critical philosophy of religion, on how it ought to ground the rationality of religion in a philosophical discourse of justification, while it at the same time contributes to making the "lived certainty of faith" intelligible, however without actually grasping this as such within the categories of philosophy (cf. Ollig 1979 a p. 338), and in a way that also opens a space for the trans-rational dimension and autonomy of religion.

Literature

Adams, R.
1997: Introduction (in Kant's Religion within the boundaries of mere reason and other writings; transl. and ed. by A. Wood and G. Di Giovanni, Cambridge).
Adelmann, D.
1994 (1968): Einheit des Bewusstseins als Grundproblem der Philosophie Hermann Cohen (in Holzhey 1994).
Altmann, A.
1994 (1962): Hermann Cohens Begriff der Korrelation (in Holzhey 1994).
Arendt, H.
1963: On Revolution, New York.
Baumgartner, H. M.
1992: Das "ethische gemeine Wesen" und die Kirche in Kants Religionsschrift (in Ricken/Marty (Hg.) 1992).
Benhabib, S.
1986: Critique, Norm and Utopia. A Study of the Foundations of Critical Theory, New York.
1992: Situating the Self. Gender, Community and Postmodernism in Contemporary Ethics, New York.
Blum, L.
1980: Compassion (in A. O. Rorty (ed.): Explaining Emotions, Berkeley and Los Angeles).
Brumlik, M.
1994: Theologie und Messianismus im Denken Adornos (in E. Goodman – Thau und W. Schmid – Kowarzik (Hg.): Messianismus zwischen Mythos und Macht, Berlin).

Bonaunet, K.
　1988: Aristotelisk eller kantiansk etikk? (in Norsk filosofisk tidsskrift).
　1993: Kants etikk og den transcendentalpragmatiske diskursetikken, Doctoral dissertation, Universitetet i Tromsø.
　1994a: Kant og Scotus om det onde (in Norsk filosofisk tidsskrift).
　1994b: Kristne element i Kants etikk og religionsfilosofi (ms., unpublished).
　1997: Deontologiske element i Thomas Aquinas' etikk (in J. Meløe et al (utg.): Tromsøvarianten, Artikler i anledning 25-årsjubileet for examen philosophicum i Tromsø, Tromsø).
Buber, M.
　1952: Eclipse of God. Studies in the Relation Between Religion and Philosophy, New York.
　1965: Guilt and Guilt Feelings (in Buber: The Knowledge of Man, London).
Byrne, P.
　1998: The Moral Interpretation of Religion, Grand Rapids.
Cassirer, E.
　1996 (1935): Cohen's Philosophy of Religion (in Internationale Zeitschrift für Philosophie).
Clack, B.
　1999: An Introduction to Wittgenstein's Philosophy of Religion, Edinburgh.
Cohen, H.
　ERW: Ethik des reinen Willens (1904), (3. Auflage, Berlin 1921).
　RuS: Religion und Sittlichkeit (1906) (in Jüdische Schriften, III).
　BR: Der Begriff der Religion im System der Philosophie (1915) (edition: Werke, 10, Olms Verlag, Hildesheim u.a., 1996).
　RV: Religion der Vernunft aus Quellen des Judentums (1919) (edition: Fourier Verlag, Wiesbaden, 1988).

RH: Reason and Hope. Selections from the Jewish Writings of Hermann Cohen, translated by E. Jospe, Cincinnati, 1993.
RR: Religion of Reason. Out of the Sources of Judaism. Translated by S. Kaplan, Atlanta, 1995.

Davies, B.
1993: The Thought of Thomas Aquinas, Oxford.

Donagan, A.
1977: The Theory of Morality, Chicago.
1999: Ethics and Theology: Two Lectures (in Reflections on Philosophy and Religion, Oxford).

Dreyer, M.
1985: Die Idee Gottes im Werk Hermann Cohen, Meisenheim.

Ebbinghaus, J.
1994 (1956): Hermann Cohen als Philosoph und Publizist (in Holzhey 1994).

Fischer, N.
1995: Die philosophische Frage nach Gott: ein Gang durch ihre Stationen, Paderborn.

Gaita, R.
1996: Is Religion an Infantile Morality? (in D. Z. Phillips (ed.): Religion and Morality, New York).

Galbraith, E.
1996: Kant and Theology: Was Kant a Closet Theologian? San Fransisco.
1997: Kant and Richard Schaeffler's Catholic Theology of Hope (in Philosophy and Theology).

Gibbs, R.
1992: Correlations in Rosenzweig and Levinas, Princeton.

Gilson, E.
1936: The Spirit of Mediaeval Philosophy (edition: Notre Dame, 1991).

Goodman-Thau, E.
1994: Spinozas Offenbarungslehre und der nachidealistische Idealismus in der jüdischen Religionsphilosophie Hermann Cohens (in H. Delf, J.H.Schoeps, M. Walter (Hg.): Spinoza in der europäischen Geistesgeschichte, Berlin).
2000: Das Gebet im jüdischen Gottesdienst zwischen Erkenntnis und Handlung. Hermann Cohens religiöse Hermeneutik aus den Quellen des Judentums (in Holzhey, Motzkin, Wiedebach (Hg.) 2000).

Gutting, G.
1982: Religious Belief and Religious Scepticism, Notre Dame.

Habermas, J.
1979: Communication and the Evolution of Society. Translated by T. McCarthy, Boston
1981: Theorie des kommunikativen Handelns. Band 2. Zur Kritik der funktionalistischen Vernunft, Frankfurt a. M.
1988: Metaphysik nach Kant (in Habermas: Nachmetaphysisches Denken, Frankfurt a. M.).
1991: Texte und Kontexte, Frankfurt a. M.
1991a: Max Horkheimer: Zur Entwicklungsgeschichte seines Werkes (in Habermas 1991).
1991b: Zu Max Horkheimers Satz: "Einen unbedingten Sinn zu retten ohne Gott, ist eitel" (in Habermas 1991).
1998: Postmetaphysical Thinking. Translated by W. M. Hohgarten, Cambridge.

Habermas, J./Mendieta, E.
2002: Religion and Rationality: Essays on reason, God and morality; ed. by E Mendieta, Cambridge.

Habichler, A.
1991: Reich Gottes als Thema des Denkens bei Kant. Entwicklungsgeschichtliche und systematische Studien zur kantischen Reich-Gottes-Idee, Mainz.

Haeffner, G.
1997: Sinn und Problematik eines philosophischen Verstehens von Religion (in G. Wieland (Hg.): Religion als Gegenstand der Philosophie, Paderborn u. a.).

Hare, J.
1996: The Moral Gap. Kantian Ethics, Human Limits, and God's Assistance, Oxford.

Hartmann, N.
Ethik: Ethik (1926; edition: W. De Gruyter, Berlin, 1962).

Hessen, J.
1924: Die Religionsphilosophie des Neukantianismus, Freiburg.
1948: Religionsphilosophie, Bd. I, Essen.

Holzhey, H.
1986: Cohen und Natorp, Bd. II, Basel und Stuttgart.
1992: Neukantianische Ethik (in A. Pieper (Hg.) 1992).
1993: Hermann Cohen: der Philosoph in Auseinandersetzung mit den politischen und gesellschaftlichen Problemen seiner Zeit (in R. Brandt und F. Orlik (Hg.): Philosophisches Denken – Politisches Wirken. Hermann – Cohen Kolloquium, Marburg 1992, Hildesheim u. a.).
1994: (Hg.): Hermann Cohen, Frankfurt a. M (u. a.).
1994a: Einleitung (in Holzhey 1994).
2000: Der systematische Ort der "Religion der Vernunft" im Gesamtwerk Hermann Cohens (in Holzhey, Motzkin, Wiedebach (Hg.) 2000).
2001: Die Religion im System der Philosophie Cohens (ms.).

Holzhey, H.; Motzkin, G.; Wiedebach, H. (Hg.)
2000: "Religion der Vernunft aus den Quellen des Judentums". Tradition und Ursprungsdenken in Hermann Cohens Spätwerk, Hildesheim, Zürich, New York.

Honnefelder, L.
1975: Zur Philosophie der Schuld (in Theologische Quartalsschrift).

Honneth, A.
1995: The Other of Justice: Habermas and the ethical challenge of postmodernism (in S.K. White (ed): The Cambridge Companion to Habermas, Cambridge).
Horkheimer, M.
1933: Materialismus und Moral (in Kritische Theorie, eine Dokumentation, Bd. I, Frankfurt a.M., 1968).
1970: Auf das ganz Andere hoffen (in Der Spiegel, Januar 1970).
1970a: Sehnsucht nach dem ganz Anderen (in Gesammelte Schriften, 7, Frankfurt a.M).
Horwitz, R.
2000: Two Models of Atonement in Cohen's "Religion of Reason": one according to Ezekiel, the other "joyful in sufferings" according to Job (in Holzhey, Motzkin, Wiedebach (Hg.) 2000)
Huyzing, K.
1995: Das jüdische Apriori. Die Bedeutung der Religionsphilosophie Cohens für den jüdisch-christlichen Dialog (in Neue Zeitschrift für systematische Theologie und Religionsphilosophie).
Jaspers, K.
1962: Die Schuldfrage. Zur politischen Haftung Deutschlands, München/Zürich.
Kajon, I.
2000: Spirit of sanctity and sanctification in "Religion of Reason" (Hermann Cohen between Maimonides and Martin Buber) (in Holzhey, Motzkin, Wiedebach (Hg.) 2000).
Kamlah, W.
1973: Philosophische Anthropologie. Sprachkritische Grundlegung und Ethik, Mannheim (u.a.).
Kant, I.
KRV: Kritik der Reinen Vernunft (1781/1787).
Prol.: Prolegomena zu einer jeden künftigen Metaphysik, die als Wissenschaft wird auftreten können (1783).

Grl.: Grundlegung zur Metaphysik der Sitten (1785).
KPV: Kritik der praktischen Vernunft (1788).
KdU: Kritik der Urteilskraft (1790)
Rel.: Die Religion innerhalb der Grenzen der blossen Vernunft (1793).
MdS: Metaphysik der Sitten (1797).
(all in Philosophische Bibliothek, Felix Meiner Verlag, Berlin).
Ende [...]: Das Ende aller Dinge (1794) (Werke, Hg. v. W. Weischedel, Bd. XI).
SF: Streit der Fakultäten (1798) (Ak. Ausg., Bd. VII).
Logik: Logik (1800) (Ak. Ausg., Bd. IX).

Kaplan, L.
2000: Herman Cohen's Theory of Sacrifice in "Religion of Reason Out of the Sources of Judaism" (in Holzhey, Motzkin, Wiedebach (Hg.) 2000)

Kierkegaard, S.
EE: Enten/Eller (1843).
FB: Frygt og Bæven (1843).
BA: Begrebet Angest (1844).
SD: Sygdommen til Døden (1849).
(all in Søren Kierkegaards Samlede Værker, utg. v. A.B. Drachmann, J.L. Heiberg og H.O. Lange, København, 1962).

Kim, K.
1995: Das Schuldproblem des Menschen in der deutschen Literatur des 20. Jahrhunderts. Eine vergleichende Untersuchung am Beispiel von Romanen Franz Kafkas, Hermann Brochs und Thomas Manns, Würzburg).

Kjetsaa, G.
1985: Fjodor Dostojevski – et dikterliv, Oslo.

Kluback, W.
1984: Hermann Cohen. The Challenge of a Religion of Reason (Brown University, Judaic Studies, 53).

Korsgaard, C.
1996: Creating the Kingdom of Ends, Cambridge.
Kutschera, F. von
1991: Vernunft und Glaube, Berlin u. New York.
Kvist, H. O.
1980: Das radikale Böse bei Immanuel Kant (in W. Strothmann (Hg.): Makarios-Symposium über das Böse, Wiesbaden).
Köhler, W.
1996: (Hg.): Nachmetaphysisches Denken und Religion, Würzburg.
1996a: "Bewährung im Leben" – v. Kutscheras praktischer Religionsbegriff (in Köhler (Hg.) 1996).
Launay, M. B. de
1992: Religion und Aufklärung bei Hermann Cohen (in E. Rudolph (Hg.): Die Vernunft und ihr Gott: Studien zum Streit zwischen Religion und Aufklärung, Stuttgart).
2000: Die Versöhnung als Abwandlung des Ursprungsprinzips in der Korrelation zwischen Gott und Mensch (in Holzhey, Motzkin, Wiedebach (Hg.) 2000).
Leaman, O.
1995: Evil and Suffering in Jewish Philosophy, Cambridge.
Levy, Z.
1997: Hermann Cohen and Emmauel Levinas (in S. Moses/ H. Wiedebach (ed.): Hermann Cohen's Philosophy of Religion, Hildesheim, Zürich, New York).
Lossky, V.
1978: Orthodox Theology. An Introduction, Crestwood.
Lutz-Bachmann, M.
1996: "Nachmetaphysisches Denken" und Religion. Der Beitrag von Jürgen Habermas zu einem offenen Problem (in W. Köhler (Hg.) 1996)
1996 a: Biografischer Notiz (in C. und M. Hauskeller (Hg.): "[…] was die Welt im Innersten zusammenhält". 34 Wege zur Philosophie, Hamburg).

Löw, R.
   1994: Die neuen Gottesbeweise, Augsburg.
Löwith, K.
   1968: Philosophie der Vernunft und Religion der Offenbarung in H. Cohens Religionsphilosophie (in Sämtliche Werke, 3: Wissen, Glaube und Skepsis, Stuttgart 1985).
McCarthy, T.
   1997: Review of: S.K. White (ed.): The Cambridge Companion to Habermas (in Ethics).
Mehl, P.J.
   1995: Moral Virtue, Mental Health, and Happiness: The Moral Psychology of Kierkegaard's Judge William (in R.L. Perkins (ed.): International Kierkegaard Commentary: Either – Or, Part II, Macon, Georgia).
Morris, H.
   1976: Guilt and Suffering (in Morris: On Guilt and Innocence, Berkeley and Los Angeles).
Mulholland, L.
   1991: Freedom and Providence in Kant's Account of Religion: The Problem of Expiation (in P.J. Rossi and M.J. Wreen (ed.): Kant's Philosophy of Religion Reconsidered, Bloomington).
Natorp, P.
   1915: "Zu Cohens Religionsphilosophie" (Der Begriff der Religion im System der Philosophie); and also drafts for letters to Cohen (in H. Holzhey: Cohen und Natorp, Bd. 2, Basel und Stuttgart, 1986).
Novak, D.
   2000: Das noachidische Naturrecht bei Hermann Cohen (in Holzhey, Motzkin, Wiedebach (Hg.) 2000).
Nussbaum, M.
   2001: Uppheavals of Thought. The Intelligence of the Emotions, Cambridge.

Ollig, H.L.
:   1978: Aporetische Freiheitsphilosophie. Zu Hermann Cohens philosophischem Ansatz (in Philosophisches Jahrbuch).
    1979: Der Neukantianismus, Stuttgart.
    1979 a: Religion und Freiheitsglaube. Zur Problematik von Hermann Cohens später Religionsphilosophie, Meisenheim a. Glan.
    1994: Das Problem der Religion und die Philosophie des Neukantianismus (in E.W. Orth und H. Holzhey (Hg.): Neukantianismus. Perspektiven und Probleme, Würzburg).

O'Meara, T.F.
:   1997: Thomas Aquinas. Theologian, Notre Dame.

Otto, R.
:   1981 (1931): Wert, Würde und Recht (in Otto: Aufsätze zur Ethik, hg. v. J.S. Boozer, München).

Pascher, M.
:   1993: Cohens Ethik im Spannungsfeld zwischen Kant und Hegel (in R. Brandt und F. Orlik (Hg.): Philosophisches Denken – Politisches Wirken. Hermann – Cohen Kolloquium, Marburg 1992, Hildesheim u.a.).

Pieper, A.M.
:   1992 (Hg.): Geschichte der neueren Ethik, 2, Tübingen und Basel.
    2000: Søren Kierkegaard, München.

Poma, A.
:   1996: Einleitung (in Cohen: Werke, 10, Hildesheim u.a.).
    1997: The Critical Philosophy of Hermann Cohen, Albany, N.Y.

Quinn, P.
:   1997: Kierkegaard's Christian Ethics (in A. Hannay and G.D. Marino (ed.): The Cambridge Companion to Kierkegaard).

Rahner, K.
:   1976: Grundkurs des Glaubens, Freiburg.

Ricken, F.
>1992: Kanon und Organon. Religion und Offenbarung im "Streit der Fakultäten" (in Ricken/Marty (Hg.) 1992).
>1995: Die Rationalität der Religion in der analytischen Philosophie: Swinburne, Mackie, Wittgenstein (in Philosophisches Jahrbuch).

Ricken, F./Marty, F. (Hg.)
>1992: Kant über Religion, Stuttgart.

Ricoeur, P.
>1967: The Symbolism of Evil, New York.
>1992 (1967): Guilt, Ethics and Religion (in S.B. Twiss and W.H. Conser Jr. (ed.): Experience of the Sacred, Hanover and London).

Ringgren, H./Ström, F.
>1972: Religionens form och funktion, Uppsala.

Rosenzweig, F.
>1994 (1924): Einleitung in die Akademieausgabe der Jüdischen Schriften Hermann Cohens (in Holzhey 1994).

Rotenstreich, N.
>1996: Essays in Jewish Philosophy in the Modern Era (ed. by R. Munk, Amsterdam).

Rudd, A.
>1993: Kierkegaard and the Limits of the Ethical, Oxford.

Röd, W.
>1999: Ist der Gott der Philosophen tot? (in H.M. Baumgartner und H. Waldendels (Hg.): Die philosophische Gottesfrage am Ende des 20. Jahrhunderts, Freiburg).

Scanlan, J.P.
>2002: Dostoevsky the Thinker, Ithaca.

Schaeffler, R.
>1981: Die Vernunft und das Wort. Zum Religionsverständnis bei Hermann Cohen und Franz Rosenzweig (in Zeitschrift für Theologie und Kirche).

1989: Das Gebet und das Argument, Düsseldorf.
1999: Reason and the Question of God. An Introduction to the Philosophy of Religion, New York.

Scheler, M.
Wesen [...]: Wesen und Formen der Sympathie (1922) (utg.: Studienausgabe, Bouvier Verlag, Bonn 1985).
VEM: Vom Ewigen im Menschen, ((1920) utg.: Der neue Geist Verlag, Berlin, 1933).

Schillebeeckx, E.
1994: "I Am a Happy Theologian". Conversations with Fransesco Strazzari, New York.

Schmid, P.A.
1995: Ethik als Hermeneutik. Systematische Untersuchungen zu Hermann Cohens Rechts- und Tugendlehre, Würzburg.
2000: Die Tugendlehre in der "Religion der Vernunft" (in Holzhey, Motzkin, Wiedebach (Hg.) 2000).

Schnädelbach, H.
1985: Max Horkheimer and the Moral Philosophy of German Idealism (in Telos).

Scholz, H.
1922: Religionsphilosophie (edition: de Gruyter Verlag, Berlin, 1974).

Schreiber, H.P.
1992: Ethik der kritischen Theorie (in A. Pieper 1992).

Schulte, C.
1994: Messias und Identität. Zum Messianismus im Werk einiger deutsch-jüdischer Denker (in E. Goodman – Thau und W. Schmid – Kowarzik (Hg.): Messianismus zwischen Mythos und Macht, Berlin).
1997: Theodizee bei Kant und Cohen (in S. Moses/H. Wiedebach (ed.): Cohen's Philosophy of Religion, Hildesheim, Zürich, New York).
2000: Noachidische Gebot und Naturrecht (in Holzhey, Motzkin, Wiedebach (Hg.) 2000).

Schulthess, P.
- 1993: Platon: Geburtsstätte des Cohenschen Apriori? (in R. Brandt u. F. Orlik (Hg.): Philosophisches Denken – Politisches Wirken. Hermann Cohen – Kolloquium Marburg 1992, Hildesheim u. a.).

Seeskin, K.
- 1990: Jewish Philosophy in a Secular Age, Albany, N.Y.
- 1995: How to read "Religion of Reason" (in H. Cohen: Religion of Reason Out of the Sources of Judaism, Atlanta).
- 2000: Hermann Cohen on Idol Worship (in Holzhey, Motzkin, Wiedebach (Hg.) 2000).
- 2001: Autonomy in Jewish Philosophy, Cambridge.

Silber, J.R.
- 1960: The Ethical Significance of Kant's "Religion" (introduction to T.M. Greene and H.H. Hudson's translation of Kant's Religion [...]).

Spaemann, R.
- 1996: Personen – ein Versuch über den Unterschied zwischen "etwas" und "jemand", Stuttgart.

Stirk, P.M.R.
- 1992: Horkheimer. A New Interpretation, Lanham, 1992.

Taylor, Ch.
- 1985: Philosophical Papers, I–II, Cambridge.
- 1989: The Sources of the Self, Cambridge.

Taylor, G.
- 1985: Guilt and Remorse (in Taylor: Pride, Shame and Guilt, Oxford).

Taylor, M.
- 1975: Kierkegaard's Pseudonymous Authorship. A Study of Time and Self, Princeton.

Thomas Aquinas
- ST: Summa Theologiae, Blackfriars ed., London/New York.

Tillich, P.
ST I: Systematic Theology, Volume I. Reason and Revelation. Being and God, Chicago 1951.
ST II: Systematic Theology, Volume II. Existence and The Christ, Chicago 1957.
DF: Dynamics of Faith, New York, 1957.
Tugendhat, E.
1979: Selbstbewusstsein und Selbstbestimmung. Sprachanalytische Interpretationen, Frankfurt a.M.
Vlastos, G.
1973: The Individual as an Object of Love in Plato (in Vlastos: Platonic Studies, Princeton).
Wellmer, A.
1986: Ethik und Dialog, Frankfurt a.M.
Westphal, M.
1984: God, Guilt, and Death. An Existential Phenomenology of Religion, Bloomington.
Widengren, G.
1971: Religionens värld, Stockholm.
Wiedebach, H.
1997: Hermann Cohens Theorie des Mitleids (in S. Moses/H. Wiedebach (ed.): Hermann Cohen's Philosophy of Religion, Hildesheim, Zürich, New York).
Wiehl, R.
1998: Das jüdische Denken von Hermann Cohen und Franz Rosenzweig. Ein neues Denken in der Philosophie des 20. Jahrhunderts (in Wiehl: Zeitwelten. Philosophisches Denken an den Rändern von Natur und Geschichte, Frankfurt a.M.).
2000: Das Prinzip des Ursprungs in Hermann Cohens Religion der Vernunft aus den Quellen des Judentums (in W. Stegmaier (Hg.): Die philosophische Aktualität der jüdischen Tradition, Frankfurt a.M.).

Wiesner, H.
1986: Philosophie und Theologie im Umbruch. Stationen der Neuzeit, Frankfurt a. M.
Williams, B.
1994: Shame and Neccessity, Berkeley and Los Angeles.
Wimmer, R.
1990: Kants kritische Religionsphilosophie, Berlin/New York.
1991: Anselms Proslogion als performativ-illokutionärer und als kognitiv-propositionaler Text und die zweifache Aufgabe der Theologie (in F. Ricken (Hg.): Klassische Gottesbeweise in der Sicht der gegenwärtigen Logik und Wissenschaftstheorie, Stuttgart).
1992: Gott und der Sinn des Lebens. Religions-und existenztherapheutische Reflexionen (in H. Herwig, J. P. Wils und R. Wimmer (Hg.): Ankündigung der Sterblichkeit. Wandlungen der Religion. Gestaltungen des Heiligen, Tübingen).
Winter, E.
1994 (1980): Ethik als Lehre vom Menschen (in Holzhey 1994).
Wittgenstein, L.
CV: Culture and Value (ed. by G. H. von Wright, Chicago 1984).
Wolf, U.
1984: Das Problem des moralischen Sollens, Berlin/New York.
Wood, A.
1992: Rational theology, moral faith, and religion (in P. Guyer (ed.): The Cambridge Companion to Kant, Cambridge).
1999: Kant's Ethical Thought, Cambridge.
Wright, G. H. von
1972: On So-Called Practical Inference (in Acta Sociologica).
Wuchterl, K.
1995: Bausteine zu einer Geschichte der Philosophie des 20. Jahrhunderts, Bern (u. a.).

Wyschogrod, E.
 1980: The Moral Self: Emmanuel Levinas and Hermann Cohen (in Daat, A Journal of Jewish Philosophy and Kabbala).
Xie, Y.
 1996: Korrelation. Der zentrale Begriff in Cohens Religionsphilosophie, Frankfurt a. M. (u. a.).
Zank, M.
 1996: "The Individual as I" in Hermann Cohen's Jewish Thought (in The Journal of Jewish Thought and Philosophy).
Øfsti, A.
 2000: Likhet, frihet, individualitet. Noen grunnleggende kategorier under ulike filosofiske paradigmer (in M. Dybvig, B. Molander, A. Øfsti (red.): I et filosofisk terreng. Festskrift til Sverre Sløgedal, Filosofisk institutts publikasjonsserie, nr. 34, Trondheim).

Index

Adams, R. 124
Adelmann, D. 25
Adorno, T. 35, 36, 147
Altmann, A. 24, 25
Anselm 20
Arendt, H. 65
Aristotle 68

Baumgartner, H.M. 18
Benhabib, S. 43
Benjamin, W. 35
Bloch, E. 35
Blum, L. 53, 65
Bonaunet, K. 20, 33, 39, 41, 83, 84, 96, 113, 120, 127
Brumlik, M. 36
Buber, M. 45, 48, 49, 80, 92, 127, 132, 133, 134, 152
Byrne, P. 17, 141, 142

Cassirer, E. 35, 55
Clack, B. 14, 15

Davies, B. 20
Donagan, A. 20, 39
Dostoevski, F. 98, 109, 112
Dreyer, M. 16, 133
Duns Scotus 96

Ebbinghaus, J. 39
Erasmus 84
Ezekiel 77, 102

Fackenheim, E. 133
Fichte, J.G. 93
Fischer, N. 21

Gaita, R. 80, 96, 98, 105
Galbraith, E. 84
Gibbs, R. 48
Gilson, E. 96
Goodman-Thau, E. 27
Gutting, G. 22

Habermas, J. 18, 21, 43, 44, 65, 69, 71, 72, 92, 93, 94, 106
Habichler, A. 18
Haeffner, G. 14, 70, 143, 144
Hare, J. 84
Hartmann, N. 73, 78, 79, 80, 81, 82, 90, 98, 100, 101, 102, 105, 106, 111, 125, 130
Heidegger, M. 25, 29, 137
Hermann, W. 48
Holzhey, H. 11, 15, 16, 24, 25, 27, 35, 38, 44, 45, 128, 132, 137, 141, 144
Hommes, U. 24, 44
Honnefelder, L. 75, 82
Honneth, A. 43
Horkheimer, M. 30, 35, 36
Horwitz, R. 67, 94, 96
Huyzing, K. 48

Jaspers, K. 61, 76

163

Kajon, I. 86, 87
Kamlah, W. 61, 130
Kaplan, L. 87
Kierkegaard, S. 94, 95, 97, 117, 118
Kjetsaa, G. 112
Korsgaard, C. 41, 78
Kutschera, F. v. 10, 12, 14, 19, 127
Kvist, H.O. 11
Köhler, W. 10

Launay, M. 35, 37, 98, 102, 103, 112, 117, 121
Leaman, O. 111
Levinas, E. 48, 49, 66, 67
Levy, Z. 66, 67, 69
Lossky, V. 127
Lutz-Bachmann, M. 10, 18
Löw, R. 20, 22
Löwith, K. 24, 114, 120, 128, 136, 140, 142

Maimonides, 30, 86, 124, 142, 152
McCarthy, T. 43, 64
Mead, G.H. 93
Mehl, P.J. 95
Mendieta, E. 65, 71
Morris, H. 98, 106, 111, 113
Mulholland, L. 84

Natorp, P. 23, 31, 48, 65, 103, 113, 114
Novak, D. 25, 27, 28
Nussbaum, M. 53

Ollig, H.O. 10, 23, 26, 27, 45, 110, 127, 137, 138, 139, 140, 143, 145
O'Meara, T. 22

Otto, R. 41
Palmer, H. 15
Pascher, M. 91
Pieper, A.M. 97
Plato 29, 46, 68, 133
Poma, A. 24, 25, 32, 36, 48, 87, 108

Quinn, P. 97

Rahner, K. 10, 76
Rawls, J. 43
Ricken, F. 17, 20, 21, 70
Ricoeur, P. 75, 80, 92, 98, 104, 105, 107, 109, 112, 122, 130, 131
Ringgren, H. 13
Rosenzweig, F. 24, 25, 45, 58, 61, 133
Rotenstreich, N. 97
Rudd, A. 97
Röd, W. 133

Scanlan, J.P. 112
Schaeffler, R. 15, 109, 110
Scheler, M. 61, 62, 63, 73, 90, 104, 105, 106, 107, 108, 109, 111, 126, 127, 130
Schillebeeckx, E. 20, 70, 126
Schleiermacher, F. 31, 96
Schmid, P.A. 69, 89, 103, 123, 140, 142
Schnädelbach, H. 18
Scholz, H. 17, 63, 135, 143
Schopenhauer, A. 59
Schulte, C. 36, 103, 110, 111, 113
Schulthess, P. 46
Seeskin, K. 26, 27, 31, 34, 45, 49, 127, 133, 134, 137, 142
Silber, J. 85